# TOXIC HABITS

*Roadmap to Rise Above, Break Free and*

*Become Unstoppable*

By

Tony Ogbemure

# Dedication

*A message to all men and women who have ever asked themselves,*
*"Why do I keep sabotaging myself?"*

*If you are a high achiever fighting invisible habits, a silent struggler,*
*or a dreamer bound by invisible patterns, this book is for you.*

*May these pages serve as a reminder that your past does not*
*determine your future, and your habits do not define your tomorrow,*
*only you take the right action today.*

# Acknowledgment

Some conflicts are unseen; they are fought in the mind, in routines, and in decisions we wish we could change. It was from that raw place that this book was born.

I stand on the shoulders of people who had faith in me when I was unable to look past my personal difficulties. These pages were made brave by the words, prayers, and unshakable faith of my mentors, family, and friends.

To every reader who dares to confront the toxic habits they have carried for too long, this book is my heart reaching for yours. I honor your bravery.

To those who have fallen but refused to stay down, who have failed but kept fighting, you are the reason I wrote this. May this book be a mirror that reflects your strength and a spark that ignites your breakthrough.

Finally, I thank God for obvious reasons: my source, my strength, my steady anchor for turning my mess into a message and my struggles into a story worth sharing.

*This is more than a book… It's a hand stretched out to every soul desperate for freedom.*

*Tony Ogbemure*

# INTRODUCTION

Everybody has habits. Some gently draw us down until we can no longer recognize the person in the mirror, while others raise us up. Not all of the harmful ones are obvious or noisy. Under the guise of ease, enjoyment, or harmless fun, they infiltrate like uninvited invaders and take advantage of our time, health, relationships, and future. It is not the purpose of this book to judge you. The goal is to awaken you. Because the reality is straightforward: it's a clue if you recognize yourself in even one of these chapters. An indication that your life has been below par. An indication that the item you're feeding won't ever feed you back. a sign that the moment to break out is now, not "one day."

It contains the most prevalent toxic behaviors that silently ruin lives, such as the thoughts you have to yourself, the food you eat, and the people and distractions you allow into your life. You'll learn how each habit functions like poison, slow, steady, and lethal, and how to break it before it kills you.

Keep an open mind while you read this. Face the things that make you uneasy. Additionally, keep in mind that every harmful habit you kick is a link you cut off from your future.

Your life is too valuable to be wasted on bad habits.

# The Purpose Of This Book

This book serves as a reminder.

It shakes you, not in a whisper, but because you've been asleep for too long and are stuck in habits that seem to protect you but are actually holding you back.

For the silent warriors, those who appear to be smiling but are actually collapsing on the inside, Toxic Habits: Barriers That Halt Personal Growth was written. For the aspirants who feel let down. For the fighters weary of beginning anew. For anybody who has ever questioned, "No matter how hard I try, why do I keep going in circles?" The purpose of this book is to reveal the habits that sabotage your progress, contaminate your relationships, and steal your time. It's about grace with grit, not about guilt. One choice at a time, you must wake up and reclaim your life.

- The goal is straightforward but crucial:
- To assist you in identifying the patterns you have accepted as regular.
- To help you express the suffering you've hidden...
- And to lead you, step by step, into self-mastery and out of self-sabotage, from failure to self-control.

Going from stuck to unstoppable.

Cycles are not something you were born to repeat. You were made to shatter them.

If you're sick of not reaching your full potential or if you're prepared to recover, get back up and start over. Then you should read this book.

Let go of the things that have been preventing you from moving forward.

It's time to reach new heights. It's time to permanently kick the poisonous behaviors.

# Table of Contents

# Part 1 – The Mind's Silent Saboteurs

## *(Habits that quietly kill your potential)*

1. **The Habit of Negative Self-Talk** – Becoming your own worst enemy

2. **The Habit of Procrastination** – Delaying your future one "later" at a time

3. **The Comfort Trap: The Habit of Laziness** – Choosing ease over progress

Each person has two versions of themselves: the one they secretly keep back and the one they aspire to be. Surprisingly, the invisible adversaries we've allowed to establish themselves in our brains are often the ones that prevent us from growing in life, rather than the obvious ones. These behaviors murmur, lie, and pass for innocuous; they don't shout or declare their demise. They gradually destroy your potential in silence.

This section of the book sheds light on the unseen saboteurs, the routines that seem so normal and insignificant that we are barely aware of their capacity to thwart our fate. They are the decisions we make every day, the ways of thinking we tolerate, and the times we compromise comfort for advancement.

The reality is that your internal behaviors are the real enemy, not the external environment. Most people never achieve the productivity, growth, and fulfillment that can be unlocked by mastering these.

We'll highlight three of the most harmful yet prevalent behaviors in this section:

**The Habit of Negative Self-Talk**:

You are your own worst enemy because of your inner critic.

**The Habit of Procrastination:**

The time thief who makes you believe that tomorrow is preferable to today. The Comfort Trap and the Habit of Laziness. The silent choice of ease over progress that slowly robs you of your future.

# 1. The Habit Of Negative Self-Talk

## *Becoming your own worst enemy*

The only limits in life are the ones you make.

And as Gandhi is often quoted,

> *"Your beliefs become your thoughts, your thoughts become your words, your words become your actions, your actions become your habits, your habits become your values, and your values become your destiny."*

A harsh truth comes out when you put these facts together: the words you say to yourself in the dark first shape your future.

The invisible enemy that resides within is negative self-talk. That voice is telling you that you are not good enough. You're not capable of it. There are better people. You will only fail. This voice gets louder with time, not because it's true, but because you keep saying it until it becomes ingrained in your mind. Your belief turns into thinking. Your word is that notion. Actions, or worse, inactions follow those words. These behaviors then become habits that ultimately determine how your life unfolds, much like Gandhi's chain reaction. Continuous self-criticism creates imperceptible barriers that impede your own advancement. Consider this: Although there will always be challenges in the outside world, the strongest prison is the one you build inside your own mind. Negative self-talk accomplishes this by persuading you to accept unreal limitations.

For this reason, negative self-talk poses a greater threat than opposition from others. You can push past rejection, defeat, skepticism, and battle doubters, but how can you defeat an internal enemy? You can't avoid it. You face it. You reveal it. Additionally, you retrain your mind to talk to itself in a different way.

Every accomplished individual you look up to has had periods of uncertainty. The distinction is that they resisted allowing their inner critic to define them. They mentally revised the script. Instead of "I can't," they practiced "I can learn." They told themselves, "I am growing," rather than, "I am not enough."

Being conscious is necessary to overcome the negative self-talk habit. You can catch yourself in the act. Take note of the words you use to describe yourself. Would you address a friend in the same manner that you address yourself? If not, you've already realized that you have turned into your own critic, abuser, and prisoner. You have to learn to encourage yourself if you want to progress. Put a voice of possibility in place of the voice of defeat. Remember that every step forward matters, even if you're not where you want to be yet. Keep in mind that you are constantly listening to yourself. Your beliefs will change if you can change the way you talk to yourself. You can change your fate by changing your beliefs.

**A Story of the Fall Within :**

At one point, a young executive, Frank, was at his career height. Being the youngest executive in his organization, he possessed all the qualities that others valued: riches, power, and status. He was viewed as a leader by his colleagues, and opportunities arose all around him.

However, Frank had a hidden adversary. It wasn't the politics in the boardroom or the rivalry outside. His own thoughts were to blame. His inner critic would murmur, "You just got lucky," whenever he accomplished something. You're not worthy of this. They will eventually discover that you are a phony. He ignored it at first. But those thoughts became heavier and louder with time. Frank started to question his own choices. He doubted everything he did, he hesitated when he could have been aggressive, and he missed chances to get even better. He started talking negatively to himself.

His behavior reflected his feelings of inadequacy more and more. He lost confidence, projects fell out of his grasp, and his leadership broke down. His coworkers gradually stopped believing in him. He was pushed down the ladder by one mistake after another until he eventually lost everything, his influence, his reputation, and his position.

Neither the economy nor Frank's adversaries were to blame for his downfall. His own inner voice was to blame. His reality was formed by his thoughts. His fate was determined by his negative self-beliefs.

*If you don't master your thoughts, your thoughts will master you.*

**Frank:** The Procrastinating Executive Who Lost Everything.

**Message:** Missed opportunities result from squandered time.

**Reset Strategy:** The strength of self-control, time management, and starting small.

**Uplifting Message:**

Your thoughts are the seeds of your fate, and your mind is the soil. You will reap limitations if you plant doubt, fear, and criticism. However, your life will blossom with growth and abundance if you plant bravery, faith, and opportunity. Keep in mind that you are the ruler of your thoughts, not their victim. Your inner voice doesn't have to be your worst enemy; it can be your best friend.

You start rewriting your story when you choose words that empower you instead of ones that degrade you. You take back control of your life every time you mute the critic and elevate the encouragement. You can control your future by controlling your ideas.

**Affirmation :**

I have no doubts. My fears are not me. My destiny is something I write. My words are shaped by my thoughts, my actions are shaped by my words, and my future is created by my actions. I rise with courage, strength, and possibility, and I let go of all the negative voices. Since I was made to succeed, I decided to speak life into myself.

**2-Minute Morning Ritual to Silence Negative Self-Talk :**

**Stand Tall & Breathe (30 seconds):**

Close your eyes, stand with your shoulders back, and inhale deeply. Assume that you are exhaling doubt and inhaling strength.

**Speak Your Affirmation (1 minute):**

Say the affirmation out loud while you gaze in the mirror: "I am not my doubts." My destiny is something I write. My words, deeds, and ideas all support development and achievement.

With determination, repeat it three times.

**Visualize Victory (30 seconds):**

Imagine yourself triumphing in today's struggles, calm in the face of adversity, secure in your work, and pleased with your progress.

The tone for the entire day was established in those two minutes.

# 2. The Habit Of Procrastination

## *Delaying your future one "later" at a time*

### *The time thief who makes you believe that Tomorrow is preferable to today.*

There's always tomorrow is a charming lie that procrastination tells. But merely a series of today's slides through your fingers; tomorrow never really arrives. Every choice that is put off is a waste of time, and every action that is put off is a missed chance.

In actuality, waiting for the "ideal moment" is the main cause of unfulfilled ambitions. Today, not tomorrow, is the time for progress.

Your dreams become more burdensome the longer you wait. The remedy is straightforward: begin small, begin right away, and never give up.

Time will never give you back what procrastination has taken from you, so act now, no matter how small.

The one resource you cannot get back is time. Your breakthrough gets farther away with each delay.

Take action instead of making excuses. Even if you only take one brave step today, you will see that action changes your life. Keep in mind that creating your future now is the best way to project it.

Life stops, and your dreams fade if you don't fight procrastination.

Every tiny action you do now opens the path to future progress. Don't wait for "someday," the instant you take action, your future starts.

A story about a young, promising man who lost it to procrastination:

## Perez's Lost Opportunity

Perez once happened upon a fantastic chance that had the potential to permanently alter his life. He was presented with a business idea that promised him financial independence and a prosperous future. He had the right people on his side, the right tools, and the right vision. However, Perez convinced himself, "I will start tomorrow," rather than acting. He was struck by the realization that procrastination is a dream killer, not just a delay.

Avoid becoming like Perez. Now is the appropriate time, not later. The instant you take action, you start on the path to fulfillment, prosperity, and freedom. Every step you take moves you closer to the life you've always wanted, yet every delay pushes your future farther away.

Take action now, as the chance you lose by putting things off might not come around again.

## The Bad Side of Perez's situation :

The tragic warning that procrastination takes opportunities in silence is provided by Perez's narrative. He lost not just money but also time, self-assurance, and the opportunity to change the course of his family's future. He regretted procrastinating and letting others enjoy the success he had previously achieved. The harsh reality is that life won't wait for you if you keep putting things off.

**Perez:** The Man Broken by Inaction and Laziness.

**Message:** If you do nothing, your dreams will die.

**A Comeback Strategy:** The strength of self-control, time management, and starting off slowly.

**How to Reverse It :**

The good news is that you can avoid making the same error that Perez did. Action is a straightforward yet effective remedy for procrastination. Now, even if it's a miniature step, take it. Make the call, write the email, start creating the plan, sign up for the course, do something. Action, not waiting, generates results.

Every time you take action, you fortify your future and lessen the hold of procrastination. Instead of waiting for regret to come knocking, take action now and make the breakthrough that procrastination once prevented.

Procrastination is more damaging than rejection, bigger than poverty, and more deadly than failure.

It does not roar into your room or knock loudly on your door to proclaim its arrival.

The whisper, "Tomorrow will be better… you have time… just rest a little more," creeps into your life.

There is more to procrastination than a mere delay. It is the slow poison that drains your energy, ambition, and destiny; it is the silent robber of dreams; it is the killer of potential. More lives have been lost to it as a weapon of inaction than to poverty, illness, or conflict combined.

**Consider this:**

Because the author kept saying, "I will write it later," how many books have died inside the bright brains of authors?

How many companies never got off the ground because someone was always waiting for the "right moment"?

How many lives remained stuck in mediocrity as a result of people confusing busyness with progress?

If you continue to waste time in inaction, procrastination will rob you of opportunities. One person is taking the risk, signing the contract, publishing the book, launching the channel, and earning the money while you put things off. Nobody is spared time.

Make regret a part of who you are. You will wake up one day and discover that the days have become months and the months have become years. A mound of "I wish I had..." will be staring you in the face when you look back.

Destroy your Confidence in yourself. You are teaching your thinking that you are unreliable every time you put things off. You turn into the one who betrays you. Procrastination is a toxic habit.

It turns dreams into dust. All dreams have a deadline if they are not fulfilled. Your vision rots if you do nothing. Not only will procrastination waste your time, but it will also ruin your life. However, this is the reality you need to hear.

You lack no power.

Every breath you take is an opportunity to start over. Even if time is running out, you have the opportunity to change the course of your life.

The remedy is action.

Not flawless. not waiting for everything to be prepared. not awaiting clearance. Just take action. The little progress breaks the hold of procrastination. Rise and make it happen.

Write the first page.

Call first.

Begin the initial exercise.

Start the initial post.

Make the initial uneasy move.

Momentum is not found; it is created. Greatness is not something you fall into; rather, it is something you construct via persistent, messy, brave activity.

Your heart's desire was not handed to you so that you may wait for "someday." You are the one who is supposed to make it come to life, which is why it was given to you.

So don't ask yourself, "What if I fail?" and start wondering, "What if I achieve more than I ever could have imagined?"

**Final word:**

Procrastination will bury you in regret if you allow it to continue. You will bury procrastination and ascend into your destiny if you get up now, even if you are shaky. You don't require additional time. More clarification is not necessary. You don't require additional authorization.

One thing required of you is action. Instead of stealing days, procrastination steals destinies. Greatness is born in action; dreams die in delay. Now is the language of success; later is the favorite lie of procrastination.

Greater courage is what you need, not more time.

Action creates empires; procrastination whispers comfort.

Excuses are the grave markers of dreams that have been buried.

The quickest way to run out of time is to wait for the right moment.

What you can only imagine is being built by someone else every second you wait. Suicide on an installment plan is procrastination. There are many unfinished books, unfounded companies, and unspoken ideas in the grave; don't add yours to the list.

Only the mover receives momentum; the waiter never does.

You can either make excuses or make progress, but never both. Starting today, someday is not a day on the calendar. Procrastination will always kill dreams, but fear kills fewer. Your future self is pleading with you to take action now. Would you? Go out there and prove it.

This is your time, your moment.

# 3. The Comfort Trap: The Habit Of Laziness

## *Choosing ease over progress*

It is the silent choice of ease over progress that slowly robs you of your future.

It feels nice to be comfortable, so good that it ensnares us without our knowledge. In the presence of opportunity, the bed feels warmer. The call of responsibility makes the couch feel softer. The blank page, the company plan, or the gym entrance that has to be opened doesn't feel as secure as the phone screen. The comfort trap is this. It whispers that life can wait, that you deserve a little more sleep, and that you can always start tomorrow. The reality is that comfort, when idolized, breeds sloth, and sloth silently destroys dreams. Those who remained in their comfort zone have never been remembered in history. It honors individuals who dared to stand up, to overcome obstacles, and to resist the allure of ease. Being lazy is more than just "doing nothing." It allows your potential to decline over time. A brick placed on the wall between you and the life you may have led is each moment you give up to inaction.

The good news is that it is possible to escape the trap. Being lazy is a habit youhave allowed; it's not who you are. It may also be broken, replaced, and unlearned, just like any other harmful habit. The life that has been waiting for you all along can be unlocked by deciding to get up, move, and take action even when you don't feel like it. You need to wake up after reading this chapter. Although it may feel secure, comfort will never elevate you. Now is the moment to combat laziness.

Discipline grows loudly while laziness steals quietly. Instead of choosing comfort that kills, choose life that expands.

You are trading your future for a moment each time you decide to be comfortable instead of taking action. Don't give away your future.

Although comfort zones seem secure, they are actually wallless prisons. The instant you take action, you become free. Laziness is a thief masquerading as rest. Don't allow it to take away your potential for greatness.

The alarm goes off. You press the snooze button. Ten minutes. Then thirty. You scroll. You promise yourself that you will begin after lunch, on Monday of the following month, or whenever the ideal circumstance or justification arises. One minor delay turns into a trend. Years pass in silence, and without much display, until one day you glance around and realize that you lead a modest life, not because fate chose it for you, but rather because you frequently put comfort above bravery and failed to see the door closing. The comfort trap's lure is that it seems harmless, unnoticeable, and compassionate, until it isn't. It's not always dramatic to be lazy. Rarely does it manifest as lazy collapse. More often than not, it manifests as sensible, courteous, and patient: "I will rest now and do the big thing later." The fear is those little layers compound that regret.

What laziness actually takes from you (the scary part).

Potential squandered in silence. Ideas that were abandoned to die in drafts and daydreams could have become communities, projects, salaries, and children's memories.

*A smaller calendar.* Days that ought to have been full of development instead become monotonous, empty, and interchangeable. Months and years feel the same. Milestones turn into "could have been" situations.

*A diminished identity.* You start to think of yourself as almost the type of person who fulfills commitments to everyone but themselves. That self-image solidifies.

Missed chances that never materialize. Many doors are one-way, including jobs, contacts, and relationships. The hallway behind you will close if you miss them.

With time, regret becomes more acute. The quiet, nagging pain that you were always destined for more, rather than the loud remorse that drives change. People wake up at three in the morning and carry that regret with them on their birthdays.

The most terrifying aspect is that being lazy doesn't feel like a decision right now. It is a sense of relief. However, constant relief eventually kills ambition. The "small life" is ruthless in its monotony and gradual stifling of potential; it is not exciting.

**Why it happens (brief):**

The brain is rewired by comfort. Identity is developed through repetition. Your identity will change to "someone who waits" if your pattern becomes "wait." Laziness is just the shortcut that leads to a tiny room with soft walls; habits are the brain's shortcuts.

**Practical, immediate, and brutal ways to fight back :**

You don't need extraordinary heroics. You need to make little, regular micro-decisions that rewire your identity in order to undermine the trap.

The 5-minute rule states that you should refrain from doing something for five minutes. That's where to start. You can either keep moving forward or come to a clean stop thanks to momentum.

Set one "non-negotiable" on your calendar, such as outreach, writing, or the gym, and approach it like a meeting with your future self.

Reduce friction by taking away obstacles like laying out clothes, opening documents, and setting up apps so that moving rather than remaining motionless takes less willpower.

Tell one person what you will do and when, as part of your accountability armor. Private action is forced by public little bets.

Replace "I'll try" with "I am the kind of person who takes action" in identity statements. Wiring is altered by language.

Appreciate your little successes since they are the only thing that can purchase sustained discipline. Encourage movement rather than perfection.

**The immediate test, Breaking the Comfort Trap:**

Do this immediately instead of simply reading it. Laziness's first cousin is reading without doing anything. I want you to show yourself that you are capable of escaping the comfort trap tonight. Here's how:

- Pick a single, inconvenient action.
- Clean the dishes in the sink.
- Put the project you have been putting off in one paragraph.
- Stretch for five minutes or perform ten push-ups.
- Don't wait any longer to send that email.
- Spend five minutes outside without making any excuses.
- For precisely five minutes, do this.
- Don't stress over how well it appears or how much you accomplish. Motion, not mastery, is the aim.
- Say this aloud when you're done.
- My comfort is not stronger than me. I choose to take action rather than being lazy.
- Take note of your feelings.
- That simple jolt of pride? Action is the antidote to indolence. Your brain has just received proof of your ability.

- Do it again tomorrow.

For the next seven days, stack one painful five-minute action per day. When you teach your body that action is your new default, you will notice something profound by the end of the week: sloth loses its hold.

The action itself is not the focus of this test. Rewriting your identity from "lazy" to "active" is the goal. You are voting for the type of person who doesn't live a little each time you follow through.

**A Call to Action: From Laziness to Life:**

Despite its seemingly harmless appearance, laziness is the silent assassin of potential. Your world gets smaller each time you make that decision. Your future grows each time you overcome it. You can either rise into growth or remain chained in luxury.

Make the decision right now to move when you don't feel like it, act when it's difficult, and show up when the excuses are loudest. Ordinary individuals become extraordinary in this way.

**This is your task, then:**

Get up. Begin modestly. Remain constant. Break yourself from idleness now, and observe how success, freedom, and progress start to come your way.

Keep in mind that a good life is created, day by day, step by step, and action after action. It is not something that is handed to you; your finest life is waiting.

Decide to take action. Select growth. Opt for the bigger life.

Take a hard look at those who are stuck in passivity; their lives are predictable, safe, and cruelly constrained. They accept less because they chose not to rise, not because they are untalented. Laziness teaches you to exist rather than to live, to live below your capabilities. It is the most reliable way to live a brief, regretful life.

However, action? The gateway to a larger life is action. You regain control each time you get up and move, even when you don't feel like it. Chains are broken by action. Confidence is gained by action. Momentum is created by action. Taking action enables you to develop, broaden, and transcend mediocrity into a memorable life.

The fact is that you cannot live a big life and be lazy. You can't remain low and get up. You have to make a decision.

Rise, Protect your life. Don't let indolence rule your future. Start now, but start small. Clean a single dish. Compose a paragraph. Step one. Every action is a decision of the better life you are entitled to.

Never forget this: activity makes life bigger, inaction makes it smaller. Only when you get up and take action will you become the person you want to be, the life you want to lead, and the legacy you want to leave.

Don't pass away too soon. Get up and live life to the fullest.

# Part 2 – Health And Lifestyle Killers

## *(Habits that drain your body, energy, and longevity)*

**The Habit of Neglecting Healthy Living** – Poor eating and no exercise, a slow enemy to your lifespan

> *He who has health has hope, and he who has hope has everything." — Arabian Proverb*

A healthy person has hope, and a hopeful person has everything. An Arabian saying that *"conveys a reality that many of us fail to notice until it's too late."* Health is more than just the absence of disease; it is the cornerstone of all success, all aspirations, and all happy moments. However, we frequently treat our bodies like interchangeable parts, ignoring the need for activity, nutrition, and care. Bad eating habits, not exercising, and burning the candle at both ends are quite adversaries that gradually drain our vitality, deplete our energy, and reduce the time we have to experience life to the fullest.

Acknowledge the battle. Life is hard. Social obligations, family duties, and work constraints all vie for your time and focus. It's easy to skip exercise, grab fast food, or forgo sleep in favor of "more important" duties. I understand how draining it may be to have your body functioning at its lowest level while life continues to move on. The harsh reality is that neglecting your health only makes the strain harder to bear. You will have less toughness, energy, and attention to work for your goals the more you disregard your body. Every iota of decision you make today, such as eating healthily, exercising, getting enough sleep, or managing stress, has a cascading impact that fortifies your intellect, rekindles your soul, and rebuilds your self-esteem. Your health is the key to unlocking your potential; it is not a luxury. Your job, relationships, and goals are all affected when you invest in your physical well-being. You regain the vitality to live life to the fullest, to do what you were meant to do, and to vigorously seize the possibilities that present themselves. I want you to honestly consider whether your daily decisions are enhancing or gradually undermining your potential before we get into the habits that steal your life in silence.

The quality of every moment you will ever live is shaped by the response to that question, which also affects how long you live. Your health, vitality, and physicality are your best allies; they cannot be compromised. Respect them, take good care of them, and see how hope and everything that it entails.

1. **Sedentary lifestyle:**
   - Absence of frequent physical activity or exercise
   - Extended periods of sitting or inactivity during the day

2. **Sleep Deprivation:**
   - Unreliable sleep schedule
   - Not getting enough sleep (adults often get less than 7 hours)
   - Poor sleep quality is brought on by either stress or using electronics

3. **Chronic Stress:**
   - Constant worry or mental strain
   - Poor stress management techniques
   - High cortisol levels damage organs and immune function

4. **Excessive Alcohol Consumption:**
   - Damages liver, heart, and brain function
   - Drains energy and disrupts sleep patterns

5. **Smoking and Substance Abuse:**
   - Vaping, cigarettes, or recreational drugs
   - Speeds up aging, damages the lungs, and reduces oxygen flow.

6. **Ignoring Mental Health:**
   - Insufficient self-care for emotional stress, despair, or anxiety
   - Ignoring emotional support and social ties

7. **Poor Hydration:**
   - Not getting enough water
   - Using caffeine or sugary drinks as a source of energy

8. **Excessive Screen Time:**
   - Poor posture, eye strain, and irregular sleep patterns
   - Reduced productivity and mental exhaustion

9. **Poor Eating Habits:**
   - Overindulgence in sugar, trans fats, and processed meals

*People who say they don't have time to be healthy will eventually have to make time to get sick." — Stanley Edward*

Despite being your greatest asset, your health is often the one most ignored. Many people lose their health gradually as a result of little, everyday practices that weaken the body, impair mental clarity, and shorten life spans. Whether we flourish or crumble depends on our diet, our movement, our sleep patterns, and even our thoughts.

Your habits either quietly take your life away or give it to you every day. Nature is unforgiving; your body always keeps score.

You are not simply feeling exhausted when you skip meals, eat junk food, ignore your sleep, or lose yourself in worry; you are gradually exchanging years of your life for fleeting moments of comfort. Health is lost in the daily decisions we make and justify, not on a single day.

Don't be shocked if your body breaks before its time if you continue to feed it garbage, deprive it of sleep, and bury it in negativity.

**Declaration on Health and Mental Renewal:**

I affirm that my health is my greatest asset, my body is precious, and my mind is strong. I decide to lead an active life, to move with purpose and enthusiasm, and to never allow a sedentary lifestyle to deplete my energy. Every stride I take revitalizes my spirit, as my body was designed to be vibrant.

I value rest as a need rather than a sign of weakness. Sleep revitalizes my body and mind. I choose calm over pressure and let go of the weight of tension. I take deep breaths every day, focusing on what I can control and letting go of what I cannot. Serenity is my way of life, and calmness is my power.

no longer engage in any habits that compromise my mental and physical well-being. I rise above fleeting escapes and embrace actual clarity and self-control; alcohol, smoking, and other substances have no effect on me. I bravely and empathetically defend my mental health. I want emotional equilibrium, healing, and peace, free from shame or fear.

I provide my body with what gives it life: clean water, wholesome food, and optimistic thinking. My body thrives on discipline, and my mind thrives on thankfulness. I unplug from things that drain me and re-engage with the environment that heals me. Instead of the other way around, technology works for me.

I am physically powerful, intellectually stable, and totally present. Every decision I make brings me one step closer to longevity, balance, and well-being. I am the keeper of my thoughts and the protector of my health. My dedication is rewarded by my body with confidence, energy, and focus.

I choose life, I choose peace, I choose myself, today and always.

# 1. Sedentary Lifestyle

- Absence of frequent physical activity or exercise
- Extended periods of sitting or inactivity during the day

Your health gradually declines over time due to the small decisions you make every day. Silent behaviors that cut your prime, weaken your body, and decrease your life span include eating emotionally, skipping meals, sitting too much, and leading a sedentary lifestyle. A sedentary lifestyle gradually wears out your power until fatigue, weight gain, tension, and depression become commonplace rather than warning you of its danger.

Your body was designed to be mobile. Movement is about freedom, energy, and mental stability, not simply physical fitness. Your single movement, stretch, and activity serve as a reminder that you are still here and in command. However, a lot of people exchange this ability for comfort, ease, or justifications like "I'm too tired," "I don't have time," or "I will start tomorrow." Until the body begins to disintegrate, tomorrow never arrives.

Emotional eating and skipping meals are two sides of the same coin; one feeds the emotions while the other starves the body. Both produce an imbalance. Your body panics, your hormones change, your thinking becomes cloudy, and your mood fluctuates when you eat erratically or live under stress. However, everything within starts to mend when you move, eat healthily, get enough sleep, and drink plenty of water. Anxiety is replaced by tranquility, clarity returns, and energy levels rise. You don't require elaborate planning or a gym. Start modestly by taking brief walks, stretching, standing every hour, drinking lots of water, and getting enough sleep. Make easy, nutritious meals and eat them on schedule. Ask yourself if you're hungry or in pain before giving in to the urge to eat for consolation. Instead move take a breath, journal, make a phone call and put healing before harm.

Consistency, not perfection, is what your body appreciates. Your future is rewritten every time you relocate. Decomposition is more uncomfortable than discipline. Your mind follows your body when you take care of it, and your vitality increases when you respect your health. Choose life above death today. Get up. Stretch. Stroll. Eat with awareness. Rest, stay hydrated at all times. Break the slow-killing loop. You are the custodian of your mind and the protector of your body; take care of both.

*I decided to move every day. I refuse the solace that makes me weaker. I will nourish my body, take a mental break, and break the bad behaviors that destroy my happiness and spirit. I start today, and I choose life.*

# 2. Sleep Deprivation

- Unreliable sleep schedule
- Not getting enough sleep (adults often get less than 7 hours)
- Poor sleep quality brought on either by stress or electronics usage

**The Quiet Killer Known as Lack of Sleep:**

Losing sleep could be seen as a badge of honor in your quest for achievement. But what if I told you that each restless night indirectly erodes your life, your ability to concentrate, and your health? Lack of sleep is a gradual self-destructive pattern masquerading as productivity; it is not a sign of strength.

It's possible to view losing sleep as a mark of honor in your pursuit of success. But what if I told you that every sleepless night slowly undermines your life, your focus, and your well-being? Sleep deprivation is not a sign of strength; rather, it is a slow form of self-destruction that passes as productivity.

Lack of sleep causes gradual deterioration rather than abrupt collapse. It erodes your discipline, dulls your edge, and makes you oblivious to your own downfall. In actuality, no desire should come at the expense of your mental health and well-being, and no dream is worth dying for.

Treat sleep as sacrosanct to prevent falling into this trap. Protect your rest with the same ferocity as your objectives. Establish a restoration-focused regimen that includes limiting late-night browsing, cutting back on coffee before bed, and creating a peaceful sleeping atmosphere. Keep in mind that while your body is in crisis, your mind cannot function.

Success is based on attention, energy, and clarity rather than restless nights. Sleep is your best weapon, not a weakness. By protecting it, you will become more resilient, sharper, and unstoppable.

Adults who routinely get less than seven hours of sleep each night are significantly more likely to develop cardiovascular illness, metabolic diseases (including type 2 diabetes), and mental health issues, says a new umbrella review of meta-analyses. (review under an umbrella, 2023)

Furthermore, a meta-analysis of 18 cohort studies revealed that those who slept for less than 5–6 hours a night had a ~9% increased risk of cardiovascular disease compared to those who slept for more hours (RR = 1.09).

You're more than just worn out. You are putting yourself in danger.

You are risking your lifespan, clarity, and health every night when you deprive yourself of the 7 to 9 hours of sleep that your body and brain require. And because the symptoms appear subtly, a little more tired, more irritable, slower decision-making, and blurred focus, you might not even be aware of it.

Don't be misled, though; this is not a typical expense of "keeping up." It's actually a slow collapse.

**It is a Warning**:

Prolonged short sleep (less than 7 hours per night) is linked to increased risks of heart disease, stroke, diabetes, obesity, hypertension, weakened immunity, impaired knowledge, and even early death, according to important research from the National Heart, Lung, and Blood Institute and the Centers for Disease Control and Prevention. This is not an exaggeration.

Think of your body as a highly efficient machine. You change worn-out parts, fill the tank, and oil the engine. However, if you neglect the maintenance, the engine continues to splutter, the parts deteriorate more quickly, and the output decreases. That's what it looks like when you cut sleep.

You could say, "I'll sleep when I'm dead," to defend it. However, you are allowing aspects of yourself to pass away too soon, including your fortitude, intelligence, and capacity for creation and leadership.

The worst part is that sleep deprivation can cause harm long before you notice it. You may still "function"—you show up for work, you check the boxes, but your potential starts to wane, your worst self emerges, and your margin for mistakes decreases.

So consider this your call to arms. If you stay up late believing you are building "hustle," realize you might be dismantling your life.

If you think trivialising sleep is okay, remember that poor sleep is **not a badge of honour**, it's a silent killer.

If you think you will "catch up later," know that while you may recover some hours, you can't fully rewind every lost night, every hormonal disruption, every impaired thought.

Let this message serve as a reminder that sleep is essential as you read the next chapters and examine the science, tactics, and mental changes.

Your mission, your legacy, and your aspirations all depend on how well you sleep as much as how well you do when you are awake.

Because everything else begins to sway when sleep is lacking.

Get ready. Although there is a lot of discussion ahead, the actual change begins right now: safeguard your sleep, take back your control, and quit allowing yourself to be ruined one night at a time.

**Sleep cannot be compromised:**

Since every waking victory you envision depends on the healing that takes place while you are asleep, it is not negotiable, even though it is optional. Your decisions, your writing, your health, and the relationships you maintain all depend on a mind and body that have been restored, cleansed, and rejuvenated. The findings are unambiguous: poorer cognition, greater rates of metabolic and cardiovascular illness, weakened immunity, and higher all-cause mortality are all associated with chronic sleep disruption and short sleep.

It's nice if you nodded when you read that paragraph. It is time for us to take action. A practical, tried-and-true method is provided below, including quick actions you can do right now, a thorough 30-day rebuilding plan, long-term lifestyle adjustments, when to get expert assistance, and references you may use in the book.

## Immediate (Tonight — start now)

Decide on a strict wake-up and bedtime. Even on the weekends, follow a bedtime routine that allows you to sleep for at least seven hours (most adults should strive for seven to nine hours). Consistent sleep is one of the best things you can do for yourself.

Establish a 60-minute wind-down schedule. Dim the lights, turn off the screens or remove them from the bedroom, and engage in a relaxing activity (journaling, gentle stretching, or reading). This facilitates your body's transition to sleep readiness.

Avoid alcohol and stimulants in the evening. Steer clear of excessive drinking three hours before bedtime and caffeine after midafternoon since both can interfere with the structure of sleep.

Create a sleeping haven in the bedroom. Quiet, dark, cool, and only used for intimacy and slumber. Simple environmental improvements pay off right away.

**The 30-Day Rebuild is a useful initiative**

**Week 1:** Establish a regular wake-up time and make sure you get some sunlight as soon as you get up. Then, gradually change bedtime by 15 to 30 minutes until you achieve your goal. Use a sleep app or a basic log to keep track of your sleep.

**Week 2:** Clean habits: Keep screens out of the bedroom, restrict alcohol and food in the evenings, and enforce a nighttime wind-down. About two or three times this week, incorporate a 20–30 minute.

**Week 3:** Improving the quality of your sleep: Take brief, early naps in the morning and practice relaxation techniques like progressive muscle relaxation and breathing. Establish micro routines around your limitations if shift work or family obligations conflict (consistent sleep window, even if timing shifts).

**Week 4:** Assess and improve: Examine your log. Do you regularly fall asleep more quickly? Do you feel more alert during the day? If not, examine resources and modify timing and stimuli. Reward successes, sleep enhancements add up.

**When to Consult a Professional: Don't put it off if:**

1. In your daily activities, you frequently nod off uncontrollably (hazardous drowsiness).

2. You may have sleep apnea if you snore loudly and gasp for air or choke when you wake up.

3. Despite practicing proper sleep hygiene, you have had persistent insomnia—difficulty sleeping or staying asleep—for more than three months.

4. It is evident that daytime functioning, mood, and work capacity are compromised.

Restoring sleep and reducing health risks can be achieved through clinical examination and targeted treatment (CPAP for sleep apnea, CBT for insomnia, and circadian therapies for shift workers).

**The Practical and Moral Necessity :**

This is more than just getting enough sleep. Protecting your ability to think clearly, empathize, create, lead, and live long enough to enjoy those achievements is the goal. No matter how admirable your intentions, research indicates that chronic sleep deprivation and disruption are associated with lower immunity, increased mortality risk, cognitive decline, and higher cardiometabolic risk (diabetes, obesity, and heart disease). Safeguarding your sleep is safeguarding your future.

**Make Knowledge a Habit :**

Create a restoration-focused approach. Start now by putting the phone away from the nightstand, dimming the lights an hour before bed, and setting the alarm at a wake-up time you can stick to every day of the week. Adhere to the 30-day schedule. Monitor your progress. Respond that sleep is a strategy when the bustle of contemporary life suggests that it is a luxury.

You don't outwork your body to win consistently; rather, you work with it. By safeguarding your sleep, you are safeguarding everything else that is important.

# 3. Chronic Stress

- Constant worry or mental strain
- Poor stress management techniques
- High cortisol levels damage organs and immune function

*"It's not the load that breaks you down; it's the way you carry it."*
*— Lou Holtz*

*"Stress doesn't shout — it whispers, and before you notice, it owns your peace."*

*"When worry becomes your daily companion, rest becomes a stranger, and joy becomes a memory."*

**The Overburdened Soul's Story:**

Many people admired him because he was prosperous, self-assured, and constantly smiling. He appeared unstoppable to the outside world. However, a new struggle started when the lights went off, and the cheers subsided.

His mind was constantly spinning with regrets, concerns, and many to-do lists as he lay awake every night, gazing at the ceiling. Sleep was now considered a luxury. Rest was alien to him, and his thoughts were louder than quiet. To get away from the noise inside, he lost himself in his job.

The things that used to bring him joy started to fade and wane. He hardly ever answered when friends called. The food's flavor had changed. Even when he sat motionless, his heart raced. His hands occasionally trembled, not from fatigue but from fear of failing.

The man behind the smile was suffocating under unseen pressure, but people could still see it. He avoided talking about how he truly felt, drank too much coffee, and browsed through his phone endlessly as a coping mechanism. His identity, the performer, the giver, the strong one, was shaped by the mask.

His body began to rebel against him. persistent headaches. Fatigue that was not alleviated by sleep. Although his doctor claimed it was "just stress," he felt deep down that it was more than that, it was the gradual worst state of his calm.

He didn't recognize the face staring back at him when he peered in the mirror one morning. His eyes had lost their radiance. On that day, he realized that long-term stress had not only worn him down but also altered him.

"Untreated stress turns into a silent poison that eats away at life bit by bit rather than killing it all at once."

**The Unseen Threat :**

Chronic stress is not the sudden rush of worry you feel before an exam or a job interview. It is far more subtle and far more dangerous. It is the constant, unending pressure that sits quietly on your shoulders, day after day, until it becomes your normal. You stop noticing it because you have learned to live with it. It becomes the silent rhythm of your life, the invisible enemy that drains your peace without making a sound.

Nowadays, many people are always in survival mode. They are constantly planning, anticipating, and getting ready for whatever might go wrong next. The body is kept tense by this ongoing mental strain, which makes it feel as though danger is always there. Fatigue, irritation, anxiety, and a gradual decline in delight are the outcomes. Exhaustion and restlessness replace what formerly felt like ambition and drive.

Chronic stress has the unfortunate tendency to pass for productive. Being busy is often mistaken for effectiveness. Because they think that continuous motion equates to progress, they run faster, accomplish more, and occupy every moment. But in reality, it's frequently a last-ditch effort to get out of silence since that's when the stress shows.

Being busy creates the appearance of control. Staying busy seems safer than confronting the emotional suffering or emptiness beneath. However, many people are caught in a vicious cycle of overworking and failing to recover due to this delusion. They feel less, but they accomplish more. They succeed but become unbalanced.

Real control comes from dominating your inner world, not from trying to do everything. It is an act of self-preservation to acknowledge stress for what it is, to stop, take a deep breath, and reset. Because stress numbs your awareness before it breaks your body. And the first step to freedom is consciousness.

1. Take a breath. Your breath is your reset button when everything else feels weighty.

2. Before you break, pause. Rest is wisdom, not weakness.

3. Make things simpler. Keep your peace like a treasure; not everything is worth your attention.

4. Give it up. It's acceptable that you can't control everything.

5. Get your body moving. Walking, stretching, or dancing are all ways to let go of emotions.

6. Keep a journal of why you are disorganized. When things feel overwhelming, writing gives them structure.

7. Sleep on purpose. When your mind fully relaxes, healing starts.

8. Refuse without feeling guilty. Setting boundaries is an act of self-respect.

9. Speak with someone. Expression reduces stress; silence increases it.

10. Don't feed your fears; feed your soul. Take care of your inner peace by reading, praying, and meditating. Feed your faith, starve your fears.

11. To rejoin, disconnect. Take a break from screens and engage with the real world.

12. Be thankful every day. Find something to be happy about, even during storms.

13. Be there. Today is doable, tomorrow is uncertain, and yesterday is gone.

14. Put restfulness before perfection. You don't have to know everything.

15. Keep in mind that you are the strength that lies beneath your stress.

**The Mental Burden We Bear:**

Small, everyday concerns that accumulate slowly are frequently the first signs of chronic stress rather than a crisis. Long after the day is over, the mind is still burdened by the unfinished work, the ongoing deadlines, and the pressure to live up to expectations. Many people are already exhausted when they wake up, not from sleep deprivation but rather from their minds never stopping.

Every notice, every duty, and every thought requires our attention in this age of endless distractions. The mind turns into a battleground for worries, regrets, and what-if scenarios. This mental stress eventually develops into emotional exhaustion. You start to feel agitated even when there is nothing wrong. Even if you are sitting quietly, your thoughts are screaming louder than the sounds outside.

Many people harbor prior scars, such as rejection, loss, or failure, without realizing how these incidents gradually contribute to their stress. Suppressing emotions rather than processing them causes them to return as feelings of worry, rage, or fatigue. There is a limit to how much the mind can process before it starts to malfunction.

The failure to establish limits is another factor that contributes to this mental pressure. An unending circle of pressure is produced by the need to satisfy irrational expectations, be available at all times, or please everyone. You gradually lose sight of your own needs as you begin to feel accountable for circumstances that are out of your control.

The fact is that a cluttered mind makes it impossible to think clearly. Space is necessary for peace. And sometimes taking a moment to step back, take a deep breath, and allow your thoughts to calm is the most useful thing you can do. It's survival, not selfishness, to learn to let go of things you can't control and to care less about things that drain you.

"The burdens we bear in silence are the heaviest, not the ones we lift with our hands."

**Ineffectual Stress Relief Methods :**

Most individuals avoid their stress instead of dealing with it when life gets too much to handle. Regrettably, the methods we frequently use to address the issue only make it worse. We numb rather than heal. Distraction is what we do instead of stopping. And over time, these bad stress-reduction techniques slowly become negative patterns.

Some people immerse themselves in never-ending activity, overcommitting, overworking, and never letting themselves rest. Others seek short-term refuge in emotional eating, drinking, isolating oneself, or endlessly scrolling through social media. These behaviors provide a short-term reprieve but rarely lead to lasting peace. While the true cause of stress is left unaddressed, they suppress its symptoms.

Avoidance takes over as the norm. We put off taking a break because we promise ourselves that we will slow down after this assignment, this week, or when things improve. However, "after" never materializes since stress feeds on postponement. It gets stronger the more we ignore it.

Pretending everything is OK when we are crying on the inside is another obvious habit of emotional suppression. Many individuals believe that showing weakness is equivalent to wearing a grin as armor. However, all unsaid anxieties, repressed annoyances, and unexpressed emotions remain stored in the body and gradually manifest as weariness, stress, or disease.

In actuality, no one can escape what they choose not to face. Ineffective stress management keeps you from living, but it keeps you functioning. Burnout, which occurs when even rest no longer seems restful, is the only result of the cycle of overwork, distraction, and emotional denial.

Admitting that you feel overwhelmed and that something needs to change is the first step towards breaking free. More awareness, not more effort, is the first step toward healing. You cannot find serenity in the same behaviors that destroy it, and you cannot mend what you keep hidden.

*"The habits you choose to ignore are what cause stress to destroy you, not the force itself."*

**The Toll of Genetics:**

Imagine being weighed down day in and day out, slowly and silently, by dozens of stones in an unseen backpack. You hardly notice at first. It's simply life, stress, and being busy, you tell yourself. But eventually, the burden starts to put pressure on your mind, spirit, and every aspect of your body. Chronic stress is a biological force that slowly impacts your health, vitality, and even the course of your life. It is not merely a mental burden.

The body reacts automatically when the mind is constantly strained. The "stress hormone," cortisol, overflows your body. Cortisol is beneficial in modest, controlled doses because it improves short-term energy, sharpens focus, and aids in problem-solving. However, long-term stress raises cortisol levels, which transforms this innate defense mechanism into a covert predator. Blood pressure increases. Sleep becomes erratic. You become more susceptible to sickness as your immune system deteriorates. Muscles tense, digestion slows, and even your brain feels hazy and overloaded. Once a temple, the body now serves as a battlefield.

At first, the results were not noticeable. Headaches persist. Even after rest, fatigue endures. There are palpitations in the heart or discomfort in the stomach. Before the day even starts, your energy is depleted. Despite the warning signs, you could continue to move forward because you think you can manage it. However, the reality is straightforward: persistent stress is a sign that your body is warning you that the load has become too much to bear, not a sign of your strength.

The physical toll is fueled by emotional stress. The pressure on the body is increased by anxiety, fear, and unresolved emotions. The nervous system goes into overdrive when there are restless nights, rushing thoughts, and repressed emotions. The effects compound over months and years, causing hormone imbalances, inflammation, high blood pressure, and even heart disease. Stress is a gradual, ongoing attack on your body's natural balance, not merely a mental state.

This is where the narrative changes, though: biology is not fate. You don't have any power. Every deliberate movement you make, deliberate rest, deep breathing, or calm introspection breaks the cycle of tension. Each pause tells your brain that you are taking back control, that life is secure, and that it is controllable. Little but steady steps count. Setting limits, writing, taking a 20-minute walk, or engaging in mindfulness exercises can help your body communicate the molecular message, "I am safe." I'm in command. There is hope for peace.

The fact that stress is avoidable rather than that it harms the body is the biggest tragedy. Awareness is the first step of resistance. You gain strength when you comprehend how long-term stress shows up in your biology. It enables you to take action before fatigue becomes sickness, before tension becomes hopelessness, and before exhaustion becomes burnout. liveliness, health, and energy are deliberate decisions rather than the result of chance. You can defend yourself more successfully the more aware you are.

Your body is paying attention. Every concern disregarded and tension left unresolved is a misinterpreted message. Your body will follow your mind's calmness. Peace is a decision you make every day, not a prize.

This chapter will teach you how to take proactive measures to regain control over your body, mind, and life, and to identify the unseen burden of ongoing stress. Because even though stress is unseen, you do have the ability to control it.

Reclaiming calm is the deliberate process of regaining it, if ongoing stress is the quiet thief of tranquility. It is more than just sleeping; it is a conscious decision to prioritize your physical, mental, and emotional health. It is the understanding that no relationship, accomplishment, or outside expectation is worth putting your happiness or health at risk for. Inner peace is essential for existence, development, and fulfillment; it is not a luxury.

Being conscious is the first step to regaining peace. What you cannot see, you cannot fight. Take note of your tense body, your mind's racing ideas, and the feelings you have repressed. You can uncover the hidden burdens you bear by journaling, reflecting, or just spending some quiet time observing your emotions. Being conscious transforms unseen tension into something concrete that you can deal with.

Acceptance, or the guts to acknowledge that life isn't always under control, comes next. Unnecessary pain results from the pressure to be flawless, to accomplish everything at once, or to control every result. Give up things you can't alter. Let go of things that are out of your control. Acceptance is allowing oneself to respond intelligently instead of impulsively; it is not giving up.

**Practical measures enhance this calm:**

Take deliberate breaths. Breathing deeply and slowly triggers the parasympathetic nerve system, which tells your body it's okay to unwind.

Get your body moving. Exercise increases endorphins, relieves stress chemicals, and gives you more energy. Even a quick daily stroll might have a significant impact.

Set limits. Prioritize your demands, safeguard your time, and learn to say no without feeling guilty. Failing to set boundaries often leads to stress.

Make sleep a priority. Restful sleep heals the body, boosts resilience to stress, and revitalizes the mind.

Engage in meditation or mindfulness. Clarity is restored and the worry spiral is broken by concentrating on the here and now.

Make connections with encouraging people. Talk to mentors, relatives, or trusted friends about your problems; stress increases when you are alone and decreases when you are connected.

Take part in activities that have a purpose. To remind yourself that life has a purpose beyond stress, engage in soul-nourishing activities such as reading, writing, prayer, or charity work.

Stress can be a signal as well as a barrier. It serves as a reminder that something in your life needs work, whether it be your inner monologue, your surroundings, or your routines. You can turn anxiety into a chance for personal development by viewing stress as feedback rather than a form of punishment.

Above all, regaining composure is a continuous process rather than an isolated incident. The more you cultivate peace, the stronger it becomes, much like a muscle. The weight of ongoing tension is reduced with each stop, breath, and deliberate decision to stop rather than react. What was previously too much to handle eventually becomes doable. After feeling invisible, something becomes visible and ultimately under control.

Mastering how to respond to obstacles is what leads to peace, not avoiding them. Being calm is a daily habit that you choose to cultivate rather than a goal.

You can regain your peace of mind and your life by committing to awareness, acceptance, and purposeful action. Even though the invisible opponent has followed you this far, you now possess the resources, the attitude, and the strength to maintain firm control, toughness, balance, and freedom.

"Calm in the midst of chaos is what brings peace, not the absence of problems."

Rarely does life go according to plan. Relationships test us, deadlines build up, challenges come as a surprise, and worry about the future consumes our thoughts. A mythological state of stress-free living is something that many individuals pursue throughout their lives, thinking that tranquility can only be achieved when all the right conditions are met. However, the deeper and more inspiring truth is that serenity is a skill that is developed in the middle of storms rather than a reward for living a problem-free existence."Calm in the midst of chaos is what brings peace, not the absence of problems."

Rarely does life go according to plan. Relationships test us, deadlines build up, challenges come as a surprise, and worry about the future consumes our thoughts. A mythological state of stress-free living is something that many individuals pursue throughout their lives, thinking that tranquility can only be achieved when all the right conditions are met. However, the deeper and more inspiring truth is that serenity is a skill developed in the middle of storms, not a reward for living a problem-free existence.

**Understand the Paradox :**

There will inevitably be chaos. Uncertainty cannot be eradicated by ambition, control, or planning. In actuality, trying to eliminate all stress frequently results in increased annoyance. The ability to handle difficulties calmly, rather than avoiding them, is the key to enduring composure. This is what it means to be peaceful in the midst of chaos: to have an inner stability that doesn't waver even in the face of chaos outside.

**Science of Calm :**

According to studies in psychology and neuroscience, stress triggers innate reactions in our bodies and minds. The fight-or-flight reaction is triggered by adrenaline and cortisol, which prime us for danger. But when this reaction is regularly triggered by everyday stressors, the system gets overloaded, leading to fatigue, anxiety, and poor decision-making.

Calmness requires deliberate effort to cultivate. Mindfulness, intentional breathing, and self-awareness all help to stop the body's stress response. They allow the mind to step back, assess the situation impartially, and stay calm rather than react. Calmness is a sign of resilience because it reassures your body and mind that you are still in control of your inner state, even when things are chaotic.

**How to Be Calm in the Face of Chaos, A Practical Guide :**

1. Stop and breathe: Your nervous system can be reset with just 30 seconds of deliberate, deep breathing.

2. Observe impartially: Keep an eye on feelings, ideas, and situations. Your troubles are not you.

3. Concentrate on what you can control: Give up control over things that are beyond your ability and direct your efforts toward worthwhile endeavors.

4. Establish little peaceful practice: journaling, meditation in the morning, or a stroll outside might help you focus on your day.

5. See obstacles as opportunities: Chaos frequently imparts strength, creativity, and resilience lessons for growth.

6. Create reassuring relationships: Trust and understanding foster calm. Seek out partnerships that promote balance rather than problems.

**The Influence of Viewpoint :**

Your relationship with life itself is altered when you learn to be intact in the midst of turbulence. Your emotional state is no longer determined by problems; instead, they become teachable and manageable moments. You start living consciously instead of reactively. Although there is still a storm, your inner compass indicates that things will get better.

*"The ability to dance in the rain with clarity, patience, and presence is what defines peace, not the absence of storms."*

**Motivation to Continue:**

The ability to keep inner peace allows people to simply survive. It takes awareness, introspection, and constant practice to cultivate this tranquility. You establish a haven within yourself where strength, clarity, and focus thrive. This is achieved with each deliberate pause, attentive breath, and act of resilience.

# 4. Excessive Alcohol Consumption

- Damages liver, heart, and brain function
- Drinking too much alcohol harms the heart, liver, job, and brain.

You can pour liquid bravery into a glass, but in the end, it will pour out your health, strength, and clarity.

Alcohol frequently enters our lives under the pretext of celebration, social comfort, or relaxation. It looks harmless to have one drink, then two, and eventually it turns into a way of life. Many people are unaware that what starts out as an occasional pleasure can subtly spiral out of control and undermine their overall well-being. Drinking too much alcohol is a steady, unseen attack on your body, mind, and future. It's not just a lifestyle decision.

Alcohol's negative effects linger well beyond a hangover. The body's detox organ, the liver, suffers from a continual barrage of pollutants, which can cause inflammation, scarring, and eventually severe liver disease. Alcohol stresses the heart by increasing blood pressure, altering flow, and raising the risk of cardiovascular issues. Your brain also suffers; memory loss, poor decision-making, and reduced cognitive function gradually erode your emotional stability and mental acuity.

Alcohol's toxicity is what makes it so harmful. Its effects build up over time and silently infiltrate your life. At first, you could think you are indestructible and ignore the symptoms, which could include relationship pressure, exhaustion, forgetfulness, or impatience. But eventually, the mental and physical costs become evident. Alcohol not only robs you of your health but also of your ability to live your life to the fullest, your clarity of judgment, and your self-respect.

Yet, here is the powerful truth: ***you are not powerless over this habit***. Awareness is the first step toward freedom. By recognizing the ways alcohol drains your energy, clouds your judgment, and damages your body, you reclaim control over your choices. Every decision to drink less, to replace alcohol with healthier coping habits, and to nurture your mind and body, is a small act of liberation, a declaration that your health and purpose are more important than temporary pleasures and escape.

The self-control you choose to exercise, not the drink you hold, is what truly demonstrates your strength." You become healthier, more intelligent, and stronger with each sober decision you make.

The effects of excessive alcohol consumption on the body, mind, and emotions will be explained in this chapter. More significantly, it will demonstrate that liberation is about taking back your life, vitality, and clarity rather than deprivation. The road to moderation and sobriety also leads to recovery, empowerment, and a future free from the habit.

**The Bottle's Concealed Cost: What Alcohol Actually Costs You :**

Proverbs 23:20–21 states that *"the drunkard and the glutton will come to poverty, and drowsiness will clothe them in rags"* in reference to poverty and poor judgment. Proverbs 20:1 describes wine as "a mocker" and beer as "a brawler," encouraging people to be foolish.

**Negative character:**

According to Titus 2:3 and 1 Timothy 3:2-3, leaders must be sober-minded, not addicted to liquor, and not fond of strong drink.

*"A bottle can sometimes keep a person's soul imprisoned; chains are not always necessary."*

**Mark Benson's Story: The Fall of a Provider**

Everyone respected Mark Benson because he was a strong, trustworthy, and diligent man. He oversaw large shipments and ensured the goods reached their destinations safely during his nearly 12 years of employment at a shipping company. His coworkers respected his commitment. "Mark may come home tired, but he never comes home empty," his wife Sandra frequently remarked. Mark took pride in being the cornerstone of his household, as he was responsible for four children.

Beneath his unwavering smile, however, was a developing issue: booze.

It began innocently. Mark would go out for "just a few beers" with his coworkers to relax after hard shifts. A few quickly become the norm. He turned to drinking as a quiet way to cope with the stress of bills, late payments, and parenting four children. He assured himself that he was in charge and that a few drinks would help him unwind.

After a demanding week, it was Friday night. The following day, Mark had promised to take his family out. However, he overindulged in alcohol that evening at a coworker's farewell party. Up until the drive home, Mark felt untouchable, the music was loud, and his coworkers were laughing.

Tires squealed, a red light clouded in his vision, and everything changed in a matter of seconds. After colliding with a traffic barrier, he was taken into custody for driving under the influence of alcohol. The damage was done, but no one was harmed.

His employer suspended him the following morning while an investigation was conducted. He lost his job in a matter of weeks. His once-proud reputation was destroyed, and his license was canceled. There was no longer any admiration in his wife's eyes, just silent disappointment. Too young to comprehend, his kids started asking, "Daddy, why aren't you going to work?"

One evening, Mark sat by himself in his living room, gazing at the empty bottles on the table. What had begun as a way to decompress had turned into self-destruction. He came to see that drinking had stolen not just his work but also his peace of mind, dignity, and the confidence of the people he cared about the most.

At that point, he asked for assistance. Mark started to rebuild through support groups and counseling. It wasn't simple. He resisted the guilt and the urges. He started taking walks in the evening instead of drinking. He went to the library to learn about personal development and healing rather than the bar.

A few months later, Mark secured employment once more, this time at a logistics training facility rather than the cargo company, where he told new hires about his experience. "One poor decision while driving can ruin everything you have worked for," he warned them. A bottle I believed to be under my control cost me my career.

His accounts served as a mirror for others. Some chose to make amends before it was too late because they see themselves in his prior errors.

## The Employee Who Lost His Job to Drinking: Mark Benson

Message: Stability and self-worth are stolen by addiction.

Comeback Strategy: Asking for help, forming better habits, and finding one's purpose will help you.

## Think about this :

Thousands of lives have been destroyed by the false comfort of alcohol, and Mark's story is not an exception. Drinking too much ruins not only your liver but also every aspect of your life, including your relationships, career, and reputation.

Alcohol's true threat is not just what it causes to your body but also what it makes you ignore until everything falls apart.

You can find meaning in your suffering just like Mark did.

It's never too late to give up alcohol, regain control, and mend what has been damaged.

Don't wait until you have lost everything. Understanding that, finding composure comes from having the guts to say, "Enough is enough."

Alcohol is often portrayed as a consolation, a means of relaxation, celebration, or escape. Beneath that transient high, however, is a cruel truth: every drink that makes you feel better actually makes you less capable. Mornings of regret, fatigue, and self-blame often follow each night of fleeting enjoyment. What starts off as recreation can subtly turn into a dependency that alters your life without your consent.

Drinking too much gradually deprives you of the things that really count: your relationships, your health, your attention, and your dreams. When you are lonely, it poses as a friend, but it's actually a silent thief that robs you of the energy and self-assurance you need to create the life you want.

Your liver, the tireless protector that removes poisons from your blood, starts to deteriorate. Your heart, the devoted machine that keeps you alive, begins to struggle. Additionally, your brain—the source of your creativity and clarity—becomes cloudy, worn out, and forgetful. The body eventually stops whispering and starts to shut down due to illness, weakness, and unstable emotions.

However, a lot of folks are unaware that drinking alcohol not only harms your body but also makes you feel purposeless. It deceives you into believing that momentary escape equates to healing, comfort equates to quietness, and distraction equates to alleviation. However, drinking actually only provides a pause, not advancement.

You are human, so your desire for peace is not weak. Nonetheless, genuine restfulness is never found at the bottom of a bottle.

Every metamorphosis starts with a truthful moment. After the party, there comes a moment when the drink is no longer satisfying, the laughter seems forced, and the silence is intolerably loud. That is your soul calling you back, telling you that you were meant to be strong, not sedated, and clear, not confused.

You have already started the most difficult phase if you have reached this acknowledgment. Reclaiming your freedom, one sincere choice at a time, is the way to healing rather than feeling ashamed. You just need to determine that your future is more important than your short-term getaway. You don't have to give up right away.

**You can begin with modesty:**

1. Your body will appreciate it if you switch out one beverage for tea or water.

2. Instead of isolating yourself, choose to connect with someone who will listen to you rather than pass judgment.

3. Re-engage in joyful pastimes such as writing, music, prayer, exercise, and service.

4. Pardon yourself for your mistakes in the past; persistence is what makes growth, not perfection.

Every little thing I do says, "I choose life." I go with clarity. Peace is my choice.

## The Benefit: Regaining Control

Being in complete charge of your life and waking up each morning with strength, serenity, and purpose is the true high.

Renewed strength, self-assurance, and purpose are the biggest benefits of beating alcohol, not only sobriety. Your thinking becomes even more acute. Your vitality comes back. Your feelings are in equilibrium. You rediscover calm that isn't acquired via avoidance and laughter that isn't driven by alcohol.

You start to view your life as it really is, full of promise, purpose, and possibility, with every day of clarity. A stronger, wiser, and more liberated person appears in its place when the fog lifts.

You become a new version of yourself when you overcome dependency, not just a habit. Someone who confronts suffering with bravery, happiness with appreciation, and purpose with self-control.

"You were meant to rise above the storm, to be sober in mind, strong in heart, and unshakable in purpose; you were never made to drown your light."

## The Internal Struggle :

Drinking too much alcohol affects every aspect of your life, not just one. It physically weakens the body that serves your goal. It emotionally alters your life and separates you from who you really are. Socially, it strains bonds and separates you from those who are most important to you.

Even though each drink can seem insignificant at first, they eventually form a chain that ties your potential together. Your relationships fall into decay, your emotions get dull, and your health is put at risk of sickness, not all at once, but gradually and silently until the person you were destined to be begins to fade away.

You can change everything. The body is capable of healing. The mind is capable of healing. It is possible to rebuild relationships. Your return begins the moment you decide to regain your clarity.

You can break free with the same energy you used to stay trapped.

- Don't wait until tomorrow or next week to begin.
- Don't have another drink; pour out the justifications.
- With gratitude, replace the glass. Healing should replace the habit.
- Every choice you make in the direction of clarity is an act of self-respect.
- prioritize strength over running away.
- Peace is preferable to numbness.

- Put your future ahead of your past.

Because freedom starts in your mind, not in a bar.

You decide you deserve better and act like it, that's when your next chapter begins.

# 5. Smoking And Substance Abuse

- Vaping, cigarettes, or recreational drugs
- speeds up aging, destroys lungs, and decreases oxygen flow.

**Substance Abuse and Smoking: The Costly Chains We Chose**

Every shot, puff, and high you get from a bottle or pipe comes with an interest rate your body and finances cannot afford."

Although substance addiction, smoking, and vaping may appear to be personal decisions, they are actually quiet debt collectors that gradually deprive you of your time, money, and health. Many people begin these behaviors as a way to find solace, escape, or even a sense of social connection, only to find out later that what was once comfort turned into captivity.

**The Physical Change:**

Each hit from a cigarette, vape cloud, or narcotic is a silent assault on the body. Smoking narrows blood vessels, damages lung tissue, and reduces the amount of oxygen, which is essential for your organs to survive. Your body eventually suffers from exhaustion, dyspnea, and hastened aging as a result of each puff. Your endurance declines, your skin becomes duller, and your risk of heart disease and cancer increases dramatically.

Abuse of substances, including alcohol, medications, and recreational drugs, destroys the liver and heart, rewires the brain, and impairs mental clarity. What used to provide a brief "high" now diminishes your overall quality of life, depletes your energy, and obscures your purpose.

**The Prison of Passion :**

It's an emotional fight, not simply a physical one. Addiction frequently presents itself as a relief, but in reality, it causes dependence. It gets harder to function without it the longer one indulges. Each high is followed by deeper emotional lows that lock you in cycles of shame, remorse, and self-blame.

You have given control of your calm to something that is gradually ruining you when your sense of self-worth begins to rely on a drink or a smoke. The moment you choose to regain control is when true freedom starts.

**The Economic Drain:**

Substance abuse and smoking are not only detrimental to your health but also steal your wealth in silence. Even while a pack of cigarettes a day might not seem like much, it can rapidly mount up to thousands of dollars when multiplied by weeks, months, and years. The same holds true for frequent drug or alcohol usage.

Instead, you may use these little daily costs to finance your aspirations. What could you do if you were to save that money every month? Create an emergency fund, invest in a course, or launch a side hustle. You could use the money you currently spend on self-destruction to further your personal growth.

Quitting gives you back your financial power in addition to your health. You begin investing in your own development instead of funding your own misery.

**The Advantages of Giving Up :**

Quitting may not be easy, but it's always worth it. Within days, your body begins to heal. Your lungs start to clear, your energy improves, and your skin regains life. You breathe easier— physically, mentally, and financially. Your self-esteem grows because you know you are no longer at the mercy of a harmful habit.

Every day you resist, you are not just saying no to cigarettes or drugs—you are saying yes to a better future. A healthier, wealthier, and wiser you.

**Pick the Better Investment :**

Fighting the habit on your own is not necessary. Give hunger a new purpose. After quitting, keep track of your weekly savings and observe its growth. Let that be a concrete reminder that the best investments you can make are your dreams and your health.

Those who choose self-control over self-destruction are rewarded by the world.

So, the question is: will you start saving to rise or continue to spend to fall? The choice is entirely in your hands to make.

# 6. Ignoring Mental Health

- Insufficient self-care for emotional stress, despair, or anxiety.

*"You're not weak for being exhausted. You need to rest since you are a human. When you choose to heal, you are powerful."*

*Take a moment to breathe before plunging into the daily bustle.*

*"I am becoming, not broken."*

*"I deserve success just as much as I deserve*

*peace."*

*"It's acceptable to feel broken and to seek assistance."*

## Why Ignoring Your Mental Health Is a Battle You Can't Afford to Lose: The Silent Erosion

We often handle our physical well-being as if it were a serious emergency. A fever makes us rush to the doctor; a shattered bone requires prompt attention. However, many of us take a risky "wait and see" stance when it comes to our mental health, thinking that if we ignore the signs of concern, they will ultimately go away. Ignoring your mental health isn't a sign of strength; rather, it's a serious danger with dire, practical repercussions.

The whole basis of your existence has silently perished.

## The Price of Ignoring Your Inner World:

A cup that is empty cannot be poured. Taking care of your mind is the job that makes everything else possible, so it is not a luxury.

Many of us view mental health as an optional investment that should be considered when life slows down. However, life seldom slows down. Emotional tension, hopelessness, or anxiety do not go away; instead, they build up. Ignoring your mental health is similar to neglecting a minor leak: it starts out as an annoyance, warps the walls, and eventually destroys the foundations.

Tending to the soil of your inner life before the plants wilt is both an invitation and a warning in this chapter. The message is straightforward but crucial: take care of your mind like you would anything valuable, since everything you value depends on it.

**A few explanations for why people disregard their mental health:**

1. Pride and stigma. Many consider seeking assistance to be a sign of weakness. Instead of risk assessment, they hide vulnerability.

2. Busyness as a badge. We value busyness so highly that taking time to care for ourselves feels like falling behind.

3. Short-term solutions. Avoidance wins in the present since distraction (screens, drugs, excessive work) momentarily reduces pain.

4. Unawareness. Until a crisis compels awareness, emotional numbness and persistent low-level stress may seem "normal."

5.  Access barriers. Many people are unable to obtain professional assistance due to cost, time constraints, and uncertainty about where to start.

Identifying these causes doesn't mean assigning guilt; rather, it means dismantling them. You can make a different decision once you understand why ignoring occurs.

## The Silent Repercussions (The True Cost)

"A life that appears full but feels hollow, frayed relationships, and shriveled joy are all signs of mental neglect that you'd prefer not to look for."

1.  Emotional decline. Anxiety, agitation, and hopelessness intensify. Resilience wanes and joy shrinks.

2.  Brain decline. Stress makes it harder to concentrate, remember things, and make decisions. Learning and work suffer.

3.  Physical symptoms. Unresolved emotional tension is frequently linked to headaches, sleeplessness, digestive issues, chronic exhaustion, and decreased immunity.

4.  Personal harm. When unresolved emotions cause you to retreat, snap, or disengage, you push support away when you most need it.

5.  Behavioral coping. Drinking alcohol, overeating, or working excessively temporarily relieves the issue but makes it worse.

Major depressive episodes, anxiety disorders, and other dangerous ailments can result from untreated mental health issues if they are neglected for an extended period of time. For this reason, immediate attention is important.

**A New viewpoint: Mental Health as Upkeep Rather than Repair**

Mental health is like dental hygiene. Instead of waiting until your teeth hurt to brush, you take simple, regular steps to stop tooth decay. Little regular mental wellness routines help you stay strong and grounded. They are constant rather than dramatic.

"Wellness is daily stewardship of your thoughts, feelings, and actions; it's not a destination you reach once."

**Quotes that Help You Get Through Difficult Times**

*"Asking for support is a sign of proactive courage, not surrender."*

*"Deep tenacity is compounded by small, consistent care."*

*"Protect your inner life with purpose; you are its steward."*

**My message to you :**

To be treated, you don't have to be broken. A crisis is not necessary to start. Take one small action today if you are sick of pretending: take a five-minute breathing exercise, write one sincere sentence in a notebook, or give someone you care about a call. That little shift counts.

Last but not the least, taking care of your mental health is necessary maintenance for a life of significance, not a luxury. You safeguard all of your connections, obligations, and dreams when you take care of your mental health.

**I'm calling on you to :**

Get started right now. At this moment. Take two minutes to breathe. Have one sincere question for yourself. Make an appointment, even if it seems insignificant. Set a single boundary. One little step is the start of a new story, one in which you are entire, present, and capable of leading and loving.

"You deserve the consideration you show others." Give it to yourself first.

Please call your local emergency number or get professional assistance right away if you or anyone else reading this is feeling extremely depressed or thinking about harming yourself. You can contact the Suicide & Crisis Lifeline in the United States by calling or texting 988.

# 7. Poor Hydration

- Not getting enough water.

*"Nobody has lived without water, but thousands have lived without love."*

*W. H. Auden*

*"Clean water means health, and water is life."*

*Audrey Hepburn*

*"The most important medicine in the world is pure water."*

*Slovak proverb*

*"Life is impossible without water."* No green, no blue.

*Sylvia Earle*

**The Quiet Dehydration of Your Life: Inadequate Hydration**

Life is found in water. Your inner flow of strength, clarity, and vitality is renewed with each sip.

down, as a result of neglect rather than excessive use. When the human body is deprived of water, the one ingredient it cannot survive without, it acts in this way.

We frequently look to coffee for energy, skincare for beauty, and pills for focus, but the most potent remedy for lifespan, productivity, and health is there in front of us: water.

Dehydration doesn't shout; instead, it whispers until it weakens you. This is a straightforward but often overlooked fact.

## The Truth About Poor Hydration

Nearly 60% of the human body is composed of water, which powers every organ, purifies every cell, and controls every bodily function. However, many people are unaware that they are always experiencing moderate dehydration. They substitute soda, wine, or energy drinks for water, failing to realize that no other beverage can adequately replace water.

Ignoring hydration may seem innocuous, but its effects gradually accumulate, impacting not only your body but also your mind and emotions.

## The Harmful Impact of Insufficient Water Consumption:

### 1. Low energy and physical fatigue

Blood thickens and circulation slows down when your body is dehydrated. Your brain and muscles receive less oxygen, which can make you feel exhausted, lightheaded, or mentally foggy. Dehydration may be the cause of what you perceive as "burnout."

Your cells are sometimes pleading for water, not your mind.

### 2. Digestive Problems

Digestion slows down when there is insufficient water. Bloating, acid reflux, and constipation frequently ensue. For a machine, water functions similarly to oil; without it, the system becomes clogged.

### 3. Concerns with Skin and Aging

When you are dehydrated, your skin becomes dry, lifeless, and prone to wrinkles. Expensive skincare products cannot replace the natural benefits of regular hydration.

### 4. Problems with the Kidneys and Bladder

Toxins are removed from your blood by your kidneys, but waste accumulates in the absence of water. Kidney stones, infections, and long-term harm are all made more likely by this.

### 5. Inability to Concentrate and Mood Swings

Mood stability, memory, and focus are all impacted by even minor dehydration. Anxiety and irritation can increase when your brain is dehydrated, just like your body.

### 6. Headaches and dizziness

Frequent headaches can result from dehydration-induced constriction of blood vessels in the brain. Try reaching for a drink of water before you reach for your prescription.

**Water is life, whether you accept it or not.**

Water is the body's natural healer and the unseen fuel that keeps everything running smoothly. Every facet of wellness, including radiant skin, acute attention, robust immunity, and emotional stability, starts with proper hydration.

"Water is a daily commitment you make to your body to continue living well; it's more than just a beverage."

## Self-Belief Nugget: The Hydration Habit

*"Every drink of water is an election for strength, clarity, and life."* Make drinking water a habit rather than a chore.

You deserve to feel alive, not exhausted, so believe this.

The most basic form of self-care is drinking water, which requires only awareness. Keep a bottle near your desk, start your mornings with a glass of water before coffee, and view being hydrated as a sacred ritual rather than a secondary concern.

Vitality is what you get when you select water.

You honor the body that bears your dreams when you stay hydrated.

## Water: The Lost Miracle

- Water is the natural remedy that the world disregards the most.
- It is the most potent, purest, and least expensive healer you can give yourself every day.
- Toxins that cause illness are eliminated by it.
- It gives your brain the energy it needs to think clearly and make decisions.
- It lubricates your joints, allowing for suppleness and mobility.
- It controls your digestion and body temperature.
- Your skin's radiance and your organs' vigor are restored.

Even the healthiest diet becomes ineffective without water. Without water, motivation wanes, creativity fades, and energy levels drop. A glass of water, rather than a medicine, is frequently the easiest way to feel better.

"Listen before your body starts shouting because it speaks the language of water."

## The Hydration Habit's Power:

Drinking water is a statement of self-love and a healthy habit. It serves as a daily reminder that you are important, that your body needs to be cared for, and that small acts of kindness can give you strength that lasts a lifetime.

- You are choosing clarity over chaos when you grab for water before coffee.
- You are prioritizing long-term wellness above momentary enjoyment when you refill your bottle rather than purchasing pop.
- You are priming your body for restoration rather than depletion when you water before bed.

## Self-Belief Nugget: Life Is Water

Each drink is a seed of rejuvenation. You're regaining all aspects of your life, not merely consuming water.

Accept this fact: You have more control than you realize.

It's possible that hydration, rather than magic rituals, is the source of the vigor, concentration, and radiance you find admirable in others.

**When you consume adequate water:**

- Your skin exudes well-being.
- Your mind is more acute.
- Your feelings level off.
- Your body feels lighter.
- Your soul seems to be alive.

**Cherish Life's Flow :**

You can survive without many things, but not without water.

Don't rush for energy drinks, medications, or distractions the next time you're feeling worn out, nervous, or disoriented. Let's start with water. Pay attention to your body.

Every drop serves as a reminder that you are still alive, capable, and a part of something bigger than yourself.

Water is life's covenant with you, not merely a gift from nature.

Drink some water. Think more clearly. Live a longer life. Because you tell your body, "I choose life," each time you hydrate.

# 8. Excessive Screen Time

- Poor posture, eye strain, and irregular sleep patterns
- Reduced productivity and mental exhaustion

**You are officially the CEO of Scrolling, congratulations**

Well done, champion of the digital era! Ten hours of screen time today is a new accomplishment that you have unlocked! When you can confidently claim the title of "Professional Scroller," who needs productivity? Your thumb is the muscle in your body that works the most, so it deserves a medal.

You've seen a hundred people's phony happiness, travel vlogs, and morning rituals. However, your own life seems to be on hold for some reason. But don't worry, you will begin pursuing your objectives tomorrow, right? Or even the following week. or after a single further

A dopamine boost when your phone pings! Someone liked your post. You are still visible to the world. Validation has been opened. The harsh reality is that the more you browse, the shorter your life is. Your distance from oneself increases with your level of online connectivity.

- Your aspirations? Behind alerts, softly dying.
- Your attention? buried beneath social media reels.
- Your capacity is becoming overshadowed by the never-ending chatter of "what's trending."

As you pursue digital shadows, time—the one thing you can never purchase—slips from your grasp. You claim you don't have time, yet your screen time app shows that you spend 8 hours a day on your phone. That equates to 56 hours per week. more than 2,600 hours annually. Just think of all the abilities you could have developed, the concepts you could have created, and the number of chapters you could have written.

However, the screen murmurs, "Stay a little longer."

And you comply. Every time.

When you glance up from that bright circle one day, you will find that while you were stuck in a digital loop, the world had moved on. Your youth faded. Your objectives have expired. And the life you envisioned, gone, due to distraction rather than failure.

So feel free to continue scrolling. Allow the hours to pass quickly.

Alternatively, put down the phone, get up, and begin living.

Because one day you will remember the life you never had, but you won't remember the videos that made you laugh.

**Overuse of Screens: The Quiet Threat to Development :**

In a world that lives and breathes through screens, many of us have unknowingly become digital prisoners. We wake up to the blue glow of notifications and fall asleep under the same light that silently robs us of rest. The screen has become our alarm clock, our work tool, our social life, and unfortunately our escape. What once served as a means to an end has now become an addiction we hardly notice.

The truth is, excessive screen time is more than just a physical issue it's a thief of dreams, discipline, and direction. You may think you are relaxing, scrolling harmlessly through videos or posts, but beneath that comfort lies a slow erosion of your potential.

First, let's talk about bodily harm. Your posture is distorted by spending hours bent over a phone or computer, which can cause neck pain, back strain, and exhaustion. Instead of standing upright with self-assurance, the body is curled in submission to technology. As the screen deceives your brain into thinking it is still daylight, eye strain becomes a daily companion, and abnormal sleep patterns subtly emerge. Your focus becomes hazy, your energy levels decline, and even your mood starts to deteriorate.

However, the true cost is more serious. Overuse of screens impairs your self-control and mental clarity. It keeps you occupied but not productive. It robs your soul of purpose while filling your mind with noise. Every minute you spend idly browsing social media is a minute that has been taken away from your goal. You start contrasting the highlights of other people's lives with your own behind-the-scenes. Artificial perfection eventually crumbles your self-esteem.

Screen addiction subtly weakens the awareness, focus, and constant action that are necessary for growth. When you are preoccupied, you cannot develop. While the world is shouting through your feed, you are unable to hear your inner voice.

So, how do you recover?

Identify the trap first. Be brutally honest with yourself. Ask yourself, "What am I getting in return?" after calculating the number of hours you spend in front of screens each day. The first step to freedom is awareness.

Then take back your time. Establish digital limits. Set aside time during the day to avoid using your phone. Instead of aimlessly scrolling, engage in thoughtful hobbies like reading, writing, walking, meditation, or simply sitting quietly. These modest actions help you re-establish a connection with the world outside of your gadget.

Next, train your brain to concentrate. Restore your sleep rhythm by limiting the amount of time you spend on screens before bed. When working creatively, keep your phone out of reach. Your willpower, the very muscle that fosters growth and discipline, is strengthened every time you fight the impulse to scroll.

Lastly, adjust your mission. Keep in mind that technology is a tool, not a master. Instead of wasting it, use it to build. Instead of draining your dreams, let it support them. The objective is to connect intelligently rather than to disengage entirely.

Not only does excessive screen time rob you of hours, but it also steals your life in slow motion. You can, however, take it back.

Every choice you make to turn away from the screen and focus on your goals is a win.

Because, until you stop developing, your potential never ends, unlike your phone, which refreshes every few months.

**The Hidden consequences**

**1. Poor Posture and Physical Strain:**

Your shoulders slump and your spine degenerate when you spend hours hunched over your phone or laptop. Today's comfort could become tomorrow's persistent back pain, tired muscles, and poor energy. A body that ought to be vigilant and active becomes stiff and castdown, locked in motionlessness.

**2. Eye Strain and Brain Fatigue:**

Prolonged screen time exposes your eyes to blue light, which causes headaches, dry eyes, and blurred vision. However, it doesn't end there; your intellect gets overstimulated as well. Your brain is unable to concentrate on anything significant because of the constant barrage of information.

**3. Unusual Sleep Patterns:**

Your body is tricked into remaining awake long after it should be asleep by the brightness from your screen. When you substitute late-night scrolling for actual sleep, you wake up tired, uninspired, and lethargic. Your creativity and productivity gradually fades as a result of this weariness, which silently reduces your potential.

### 4. Time Wasters and Lost Focus:

You lose out on crafting your own story every time you consume someone else's product. While your objectives remain unaltered, time passes silently, with days turning into weeks and weeks into months. The screen gives you fleeting joy but robs you of long-term satisfaction.

### The Clear Message:

Distraction and growth are incompatible. When your thoughts are always elsewhere, you cannot strive for excellence. Your dreams get farther away with each scroll that doesn't fulfill your purpose.

### Ways to Recover and Develop:

### 1. Admit the truth.

Examine how much time you spend on screens. Check the status of your hours. The primary treatment for blindness is awareness. What you don't face, you can't alter.

### 2. Create Screen-Free Routines:

Do not use your phone at the beginning or end of the day. Spend your first and last 30 minutes in stillness, praying, planning, or pondering. Before the world starts screaming for your attention, give your mind some space.

### 3. Redesign Your Space:

When working or creating, keep your phone out of sight. Turn off pointless alerts. Make it difficult to be distracted and simple to be productive.

### 4. Replace rather than only remove:

Leaving a void won't help you break a habit. Instead of scrolling, try reading, writing, going for a walk, or working out. Instead of gossip, feed your mind with progress.

### 5. Get back in touch with reality:

Take some time to go outside. Engage in in-person discussions. Discover again what it means to live an unfettered life. There is more happiness in the actual world than any post could convey.

### 6. Establish Purposeful Boundaries:

Make deliberate use of your gadgets to learn, create, or establish meaningful connections. The aim is to redefine your relationship with technology, not reject it.

### This is for you, buddy:

The purpose of screens was to educate, not to confine. They open doors when utilized properly. They steal fates when abused.

You reinvest in your development every minute you take away from your screen.

Spend your time where it matters because it is your life.

# 9. Poor Eating Habits

- Overindulgence in sugar, trans fats, and processed meals

*"Eat to fuel your body, not to feed your emotions."*
*Unknown*

*"Eat to stay alive or eat to die."*
*Tony Ogbemure*

## Bad Eating Practices: The Slow Poison You Give Yourself:

Food is supposed to sustain, nourish, and nurture life, yet for many, it has become the very thing that destroys it. We suffer from a lack of discipline despite living in a time of plenty. There is something processed, sugary, or fried around every corner—short-term gratification that causes long-term harm. Your everyday dietary decisions are scripting your health narrative, line by line, even if you are unaware of it.

## The Modern Overindulgence Trap:

Overindulgence in processed foods, sugar, and trans fats has turned into a silent epidemic. "Convenient" foods are on the shelves, and the more we eat them, the less we appreciate the flavors of genuine food. While our bodies beg for natural sustenance, our mouths want for the artificial. We don't eat for purpose; we eat to satisfy our emotions.

The brutal but plain truth is that every mouthful either promotes death or feeds life.

**The Impact of Poor Eating:**

## 1. Weight Gain and Obesity:

Your system is overloaded by those greasy fries, creamy sauces, and sugar-filled drinks, which do more than just satisfy your hunger. Processed foods are high in calories but low in nutrients. Your body stores the extra energy as fat, which causes obesity, a condition that increases the risk of diabetes, heart disease, and chronic fatigue.

## 2. Diseases That Steal Your Tomorrow:

Consuming junk food, refined sugar, and trans fats regularly raises your chances of heart failure, cancer, stroke, and hypertension. Rarely do these illnesses manifest suddenly; instead, they develop gradually, day by day, meal by meal, until it's too late.

## 3. Sleep Disorders and Snoring:

Acid reflux, weight increase around the neck, and respiratory strain are all consequences of poor nutrition that can lead to snoring and sleep apnea. An exhausted body eventually leads to an unproductive life, and a restless night results in a fatigued morning.

## 4. Diminished vitality and Mental Fog:

Eating poorly depletes your vitality and impairs your ability to think clearly. You get grumpy and unproductive when you consume too much sugar, which causes spikes and crashes. You are operating but not thriving; you are alive but not awake.

### 5. The Possibility of an Early Death:

Slow self-destruction is the long-term result of persistently eating poorly. Diets heavy in processed foods and sugars have been found to reduce life expectancy. Every unhealthy meal is essentially a quiet contract with early death, sealed with appetite and signed with a fork.

### The True Meaning in Each Bite :

Your body powers your purpose. It will ultimately decompose if you feed it with garbage. No matter how lofty your goals are, a sick body prevents you from achieving them. A guy will always be a slave to his appetites if he is unable to regulate his appetite.

In addition to being unhealthy, thoughtless eating is self-destruction masquerading as enjoyment. The body maintains a score. You can temporarily avoid the mirror, but you won't be able to avoid the repercussions indefinitely.

### A Call to Take Control :

If your physical health is failing, you cannot develop financially, mentally, or spiritually. Since energy is life, every successful person cherishes it. When your body is constantly fighting the effects of inadequate nutrition, it is impossible to concentrate.

It's time to regain authority. Discipline, not famine. Through awareness, not blame.

**Moving forward :**

1.   Rebuild Your Plate. Limit processed snacks, fried meals, and sugar. Lean proteins, fruits, veggies, and whole grains can take their place. Your body feels more alive when you eat more natural foods.

2.   Make an effort to stay hydrated by consuming more water and fewer sugar-filled beverages. Water supports all of your body's cells and purifies your system. Recall that although water brings life, soda gives pleasure.

3.   Prepare More, Purchase Less: Fast food gradually robs you of your health. When you can, prepare your meals. You can rediscover the meaning of true sustenance through cooking.

4.   Manage Your Portions: When you eat too much, even healthy food can become detrimental. Eat until you are content, not overfed. Nourishment, not indulgence, is the aim.

5.   Prioritize Your Health: You cannot purchase a new body. Think of it as your most important investment. Even the biggest dreams will fade in the absence of health.

## Final Advice and Encouragement

Your condition will determine your destiny, not just your aspirations. Every good decision is a vote for life, and every unwise bite is a vote for illness.

Avoid exchanging long-term harmony for transient enjoyment.

Don't allow food to shorten a life that may have been prolonged by discipline. Self-control is the first step on the road to greatness, and it starts on your plate. Because your body may fail you tomorrow if you ignore it today.

# Part 3 – Relationship And Life Drainers

## *(Habits that damage trust, love, and your future)*

1.  **The Habit of Disrespect & Disregard, entitlement mentality, lies and cheating in Relationships** – How silent wounds kill love

2.  **The Habit of Gossip & Idle Talk** – Wasting words, wasting trust

3.  **The Habit of Keeping Grudges** – Carrying poison and calling it justice

4.  **The Habit of Entertaining Toxic People** – Inviting chaos into your life

5   **The Habit of Social Media Addiction** – Trading presence for pixels

6   **The Habit of Impulsive Spending** – When your wallet has no brakes

Certain behaviors not only negatively impact your relationship but also silently drain the life out of it. Quiet destroyers that erode trust and poison love include persistent lying, emotional neglect, poor communication, pride, and selfishness. The relationship starts to suffer from the inside out when you prioritize ego over empathy or silence above sincerity.

Honesty, respect, and constancy are the foundations of love; blame, neglect, and secrecy kill it. These behaviors are dangerous because they gradually sniff the life out of the relationship. Your peace of mind, your confidence, and ending the relationships suddenly are readily possible.

**The Secret killers :**

"In a relationship, bad habits are like termites, they eat away at love until nothing is left."

Lesson: *Small cracks will eventually turn into heartbreaks, therefore don't ignore them. Get better quickly.*

**Pride Does Not Lead to Power:**

"More relationships are destroyed by pride, silence, and ego than by infidelity, don't let them become habits."

Lesson: *What quiet destroys, communication preserves. Talk instead of assuming.*

**Patterns, Not People:**

"Unresolved problems turn into habits, and those habits ruin the relationship you once treasured."

Lesson: *Sometimes it's your pattern, not your partner's.*

**Narcissistic love:**

"A relationship based on one person's ego will ultimately fall apart due to its own weight."

Lesson: *True love is about balance, understanding, and respect rather than dominance or  pride.*

**The Impoliteness of Flirting:**

"Flirting with others while in a relationship is not harmless, it's emotional betrayal dressed as charm."

Lesson: *Respect is the highest form of love. When you make yourself too accessible to others, you make your partner feel replaceable and that's how trust dies.*

**Make changes or Lose:**

"Love necessitates change; if you don't change your ways, you will learn to live alone."

Lesson: Someone's absence is typically the cost of stubbornness.

There are two forces in every relationship: those that strengthen it and those that weaken it. Unfortunately, the majority of people continue to engage in harmful behaviors that gradually erode trust and love. Apology is replaced by pride. Lies replace honesty. Loyalty is replaced with flirting. Empathy is replaced by narcissism. Additionally, emotional neglect takes the place of effort.

These are not insignificant errors; they are silent killers of harmony, decency, and interpersonal relationships. Unchecked, they cause partners to become strangers and their passion to become icy.

It's time to acknowledge that bad habits kill love rather than dying organically.

Let's reveal the drainers that silently ruin what would have endured forever.

**The Red Flags Ignored in the Name of Love: The Beautiful Lies:**

It appeared to be a work of art at first.

When they first met at work, Ethan and Mariah had rather different personalities, one calm and collected, the other lively and free-spirited. There was no denying their chemistry. They developed an unbreakable rhythm, communicated late into the night, and laughed after hard workdays. Love and laughter prevailed over pride, conflict, and ego.

Mariah appreciated his calm strength, and Ethan appreciated her self-assurance. He showed her faith by offering her a place to stay, which went beyond simple comfort. He opened his space, handed her his house key, and unintentionally widened his heart even more.

But when respect wanes, love shifts.

Cracks started to appear gradually. It began to feel more like competition than partnership. Bold and smart, Mariah projected a sense of pride that made making apologies challenging. Despite his composure, Ethan was just as impatient. Peace is lost when pride collides with pride.

Arguments became frequent. I apologize for disappearing. Gratitude disappeared. Ethan would manage the bills, pay for rides, and buy groceries, but the words "thank you" seemed alien to him.

The woman who had previously treasured his company now behaved as though he owed her everything.

Ethan saw something worse at work: flirting. Mariah's energy changed, her focus dispersed, and her laughter resonated with other males. "They are just colleagues," she said, dismissing him when he confronted her. Avoid feeling uneasy. However, disrespect was the issue, not insecurity.

One man in particular started spending a lot of time with her. The discussions, the looks, the trips home. Ethan noticed a pattern. She ignored him, proud and in denial, when he mentioned it.

She remarked, "He's not even my type." "He is merely a friend."

However, people lie, not act. In the hopes that she might change, Ethan remained patient. However, her behavior became more hostile. She was physically there but emotionally unavailable to him. That's how narcissistic love operates: it consumes your silence and drains your energy.

Then came the night that proved it all. Ethan witnessed her sneaking into the same man's car—the one who was "not her type" — after work. She lied once more when questioned, claiming, He's just giving me a ride.

That was the final straw.

She went back to Ethan's house the following day, set the key on the bed, and left without saying anything. No resolution. No regret. Just neglect veiled in pride.

A few days later, Ethan witnessed her riding with the same man, laughing, and acting as if nothing had happened when they arrived at work.

The deceit, disrespect, and falsehoods were more painful than the separation. the knowledge that long before she physically left, the person he trusted and granted room to had already emotionally checked out.

However, Ethan refrained from fighting. He didn't plead. He turned his conditions into motivation. He reclaimed his calm, focused on his side business, and proceeded quietly; there was no drama, no retaliation. Because some endings are preventive rather than retaliatory

**Ethan and Mariah the two who were broken by lies and disrespect:**

Message: Message: Love dies in the absence of honesty and manners.

Communication, humility, and emotional maturity are all part of the comeback strategy.

**Summary from the this Story:**

1. Disrespect speaks louder than words, and once it starts, love starts to die.

2. Because pride obstructs healing and obscures the truth, it kills more quickly than betrayal.

3. It is emotional cheating to flirt while you are committed since it undermines your partner's confidence.

4. Someone has already begun to take you for granted when they stop expressing gratitude.

Love may withstand obstacles, distance, and differences, but it cannot withstand disrespect. Disrespect, entitlement, cheating and lying are habits that will always cause love to develop into hatred.

Walking away is sometimes a sign of strength rather than weakness.

# 1. The Habit Of Disrespect & Disregard, Entitlement Mentality, Lies And Cheating In Relationships

## *How Silent Wounds Kill Love*

**The Disrespect & Mistreatment Habit: How Silent Burns Destroy Love:**

The hope of enduring love is the foundation of every relationship. The daily texts that say, "I care about you," the love, and the laughing. However, with time, little things like arrogance, disregard, entitlement, lying, and cheating may start to appear. These are silent wounds that slowly drain love until the heart is numb; they are not noisy destroyers.

**Love's Slow Death:**

Shouting and screams are not the only forms of disrespect. Sometimes it takes the form of downplaying your partner's efforts, dismissing their sentiments, or continuously demonstrating your correctness. It's in how someone leaves a potentially helpful interaction.

Disregard is the death of gratitude, the disappearance of "thank you" and "I'm sorry." One partner starts to feel unseen. And the first step toward emotional detachment is being invisible.

Cheating and lying don't necessarily start with physical acts. They frequently begin with minor emotional betrayals, such as concealing your true feelings, comparing your partner in private, or making a deep confession to someone else. Like glass, trust never shines the same after it has been fractured.

**The mentality of entitlement:**

Entitlement, or the silent belief that one should be loved without effort, forgiven without change, and tolerated without responsibility, is one of the worst toxins in modern relationships.

One-sided love kills the foundation. The relationship turns into a taxing struggle, regardless of how much one person contributes.

Mariah and Ethan discovered this lesson too late. Passion and common dreams marked the beginning of their love. But eventually, Mariah's emotional retreat and Ethan's arrogance turned into quiet conflicts. Everyone thought they were the "better" one. Assumptions spread and apologies became uncommon. Love gradually died, leaving only bitterness; it didn't end in a single day.

**The Cost of These Behaviors:**

These behaviors harm one's self-worth and destroy relationships. An infinite giver starts to feel inadequate. The manipulator starts to lose their moral character. Everyone loses, even those who believe they have "won" a dispute.

Love is a living entity. Lies, pride, and disrespect are like poison poured into its roots. The most attractive garden eventually fades.

**Proceeding: Restoration and Healing:**

When people stop avoiding the truth, healing begins. Admitting that you were mistaken requires humility. I caused harm to a loved one. However, humility is power.

Whether in the same relationship or in a different stage of life, it makes repair possible.

Learn and forgive at the same time. Forgive to grow, not to forget. Accept accountability. Admit your habits, face your entitlement, and be accountable for your flaws. Talk honestly. Honesty is the foundation for rebuilding trust; silence is the breeding ground for miscommunication. Have enough self-love to avoid being disrespected. Being correct isn't always preferable to peace.

**The Benefit of Growing Up:**

You will not only attract better people when you break free from poisonous patterns, but you also become one.

Love becomes more on understanding and less on ego. You discover that honesty, respect, and tranquility are more romantic than promises or flowers.

**Perspective and Conclusion:**

Most people blame the other person when their love wanes. However, healing starts when you ask yourself, "What habit did I allow to grow in me that killed the love I once had?" as you glance into the mirror.

Silent wounds cause love to die; it doesn't happen overnight. The ones brought on by unsaid words, broken vows, and hearts too arrogant to apologize

Additionally, forgiveness is still possible even if you were the one who caused the harm. Self-awareness is beautiful because it enables you to reclaim what pride once destroyed. Every apology heals something within you, every attempt at personal development, and every love-filled truth.

## Key actions to Recover and Proceed

Take responsibility for what you do. Denial is the first step toward no healing. Acknowledge the role that your behavior or toxicity played.

With dignity, detach. To demonstrate your loyalty, you don't have to remain in a place where you are treated disrespectfully. The loudest way to show self-respect is to walk away.

Realize your emotional limits. You shouldn't give your heart to everyone. Plant your energy only in rich soil to preserve it like a priceless seed.

Growth should replace bitterness. Allow pain to motivate you. If you don't want to remain broken, the same love that broke you can give you strength.

Make respect for your new vocabulary. In romantic relationships, friendships, or family, use words that promote healing rather than harm.

**The Prize:**

You become a better version of yourself, one who loves with clarity rather than desperation when you overcome disrespect and dishonesty.

You turn into the healed one, the one who draws peace instead of pursuing conflict.

And the purest kind of love is peace, my friend.

Toxic habits destroy love, yet what life once shattered is repaired by honesty, decency, and humility.

Wasting Words, Wasting Trust: The Habit of Gossip and Idle Talk

*"Wise people speak because they have something to say; fools speak because they have to say something."*
*Plato*

Words have great power. They can burn or build bridges. They have the power to break or mend hearts. However, words lose significance when they become meaningless. And nowhere is it riskier than the tendency of idle chatter and gossip, which wastes time, undermines trust, and postpones fate.

Conversations spread more quickly than facts in the world we live in. Before speaking, people don't check. They reveal secrets, tell tales, and start rumors, often for amusement, attention, or retaliation. Many people are unaware that every thoughtless phrase we say has unforgettable implications.

# 2. The Habit of Gossip & Idle Talk

## *Wasting words, wasting trust*

Gossip always begins slowly, with an unimportant "Did you hear what happened?" or a whisper, but it quickly spreads. It sows discord, shatters friendships, and ruins reputations.

The attitude driving gossip, the need to feel superior, relevant, or amused at the price of another person's quietness is more damaging than the story itself.

Even though idle talk seems innocent, it wastes time, which is something you can never get back.

Additionally, gossip wastes trust, which is worse.

People stop trusting you with their truth once they discover that you spread rumors about others. They reserve their words yet smile while you are around.

Every time you breach someone's trust, your credibility dies.

**The Reasons Behind Gossip:**

For several reasons, including boredom, unease, jealousy, or the fear of being forgotten, people engage in gossip. It creates a false sense of significance to talk about other people. Even when that connection is based on someone else's failure, it gives people a sense of belonging.

In actuality, though, those who are genuinely developing don't have time for rumors.

They are too preoccupied with developing themselves, creating something worthwhile, or reaching new heights.

Ideas are the dialogue of the advanced; gossip is the conversation of the stagnant.

**Silent Time Thief: Idle Talk:**

The calmer relative of gossip is idle talking. Sometimes it's just empty, not malicious. It adds nothing but noise to fill the void.

It's the never-ending whining, pointless talk, and pointless disputes on social media. You become distracted from your vision by idle talks. It keeps you occupied but ineffective. You are arguing while others are making. You are speaking while others are moving.

Keep in mind this fact:

**Keeping Your Mouth Safe and Protecting Your Goals:**

Words are seeds. Every word you say plants either poison or cure. You will begin to treat your mouth like a garden rather than a trash can as soon as you recognize that.

**Here's how to get over idle chatter and gossip:**

Before you speak, take a moment. Do you think this is true? Is it considerate? Is it required?

Don't talk about those who aren't there. Change the subject if they aren't present to defend themselves.

Shift discussions. Transform negative discussion into constructive discourse. "What are you working on?" should be used instead of "Did you hear?"

Build using words. Talk about ideas, encouragement, and affirmations. When you speak, inspire others.

When it's necessary, leave. Silence is preferable to meaningless words.

**When Gossip Turn Against You:**

"If they gossip to you, they will gossip about you" is an old proverb. Those who bring the secrets of others to your table will eventually serve yours at someone else's. Every gossiper eventually succumbs to their own habit. Relationships break down when trust is lost. Opportunities disappear when credibility is lost. Broken confidence does not lead to long-term success.

**The Benefits of Meaningful Conversations:**

Instead of gossiping, mature minds share knowledge. They discuss business, love, purpose, growth, plans, and ideas. They talk about how to rise instead of wasting words on who failed. Healing, understanding, and creativity are all brought about by great discussions. Instead of slandering, they make people feel seen. Instead of hatred, they show warmth.

**So ask yourself:**

- Are my words constructive or destructive?
- When I speak, do people feel terrified or safe?

- Do I have a reputation for grace or gossip?

Your presence becomes a blessing when you start using your words intentionally. Your voice will be sought for since it promotes harmony rather than conflict.

**Proceeding:**

- Instead of using your words to burn people, let them be a source of light.
- Give up spending your breath on things that don't help you develop.
- Every statement should have a purpose, and every discussion should be fruitful.
- Prioritize substance above drama. Silence is preferable to defamation.
- Because wisdom repairs while gossip destroys.

**And keep in mind:**

What you say about other people says more about you than it ever will about them.

Your destiny is too great to be reduced to meaningless talk, therefore speak life, nurture trust, and safeguard your energy.

# 3. The Habit Of Keeping Grudges

## *Carrying Poison And Calling It Justice*

*"Small minds discuss people, average minds discuss events, but great minds discuss ideas."*

**Eleanor Roosevelt**

Certain wounds are invisible. Beneath smiles, laughter, and bustling, they are scars left by resentment. Grudges feel justified. "They hurt me, so I will never forgive," they mutter. They claim you are standing up for justice if you remain furious. To be honest, though, harboring resentment is like carrying poison under the guise of medicine.

Emotional self-sabotage is what a grudge is. It makes you believe that you are punishing someone else when, in fact, you are just punishing yourself.

**The Myth of Justice:**

Your mind seeks justice when someone offends you; it wants revenge, resolution, or, at the very least, an apology. However, the heart uses bitterness as armor when such things never happen. You feel the offense, examine the specifics, and silently hope that person suffers.

However, most individuals are unaware that resentment traps your emotions rather than your adversaries.

Your body remembers what they did every time you think about it. Your joy diminishes, your energy declines and your calm reduces. You are still playing the role of the offender in your life movie, even though the offender may have forgotten.

Grudges keep you confined to times that don't merit your attention, much like mental handcuffs.

## Feeding the Bitterness: The Lie Cycle:

Gossip becomes fuel when you harbor bitterness.

Gossip begins as a lighthearted discussion, a time for venting, but it gradually develops into a vicious circle of indignation.

You share your experience to win people over, but each time you do so, the pain is reopened. They take up more room in your heart the more you talk about them. Gossip is the recycling of emotions, transforming old suffering into fresh toxins.

Additionally, you hinder your own development when you talk about people rather than ideas.

Eleanor Roosevelt's quotation is ageless because of this:

"Big minds talk about ideas; small minds talk about people."

You lose purpose when you talk about other people. Ideas are developed through discussion.

## Progress and Bitterness Can't Coexist:

You hinder your own progress every time you harbor resentment. Looking backward prevents you from moving forward.

Building your ambition, launching your business, publishing your book, or improving your health may all be accomplished with the same amount of energy as remembering who wronged you.

- People who harbor resentment often experience stagnation.
- They stop being creative. Their happiness fades.
- Because a beautiful future cannot be produced by a bitter heart.
- When you do, life moves.

However, life will abandon you if you don't let go of the past.

**The Path to Freedom: Forgiveness:**

Pretending that the suffering never occurred is not the definition of forgiveness. It does not imply that the other person was correct. It indicates that you will not let suffering dictate your destiny.

- Forgiveness is a sign of strength, not weakness.
- Saying, "You no longer control how I feel," requires guts.
- You cleanse your thoughts when you forgive.
- You make room for happiness, fresh chances, and deep connections.
- You don't need an apology from the person who wounded you to get better.
- You are capable of healing your own wounds. Without their consent, you can decide to be whole.

**How to Let Go of Your Grudge:**

1. Accept the pain. What you suppress cannot be healed. Give it a name, confront it, and choose to let it go.

2. Don't practice. Don't tell the story again. The wound is kept alive by each recurrence.

3. Growth discussion should take the place of gossip. Talk on your objectives rather than your complaints. Talk about solutions rather than problems or scandals.

4. Instead of responding, thinking or praying. More healing will come from peaceful, quiet times than from hours of venting.

5. Honor your recovery. You get stronger when you forgive, not weaker. It is evidence that your peace of mind is no longer on sale.

**The Impact of Peace:**

When you eventually let go of the grudge, you experience a sense of peace.

After years of suffocating, it's like taking a deep breath. Your thoughts become clear. Your heart lightens. Suddenly, you understand that justice is about release rather than retaliation. You begin investing in your own serenity instead of trying to make other people pay. You begin to create what strengthens you instead of discussing what damaged you. People with strong emotions act in this way.

Instead of depleting energy on rumors about the past, they concentrate on building their future.

**Meditation:**

- You cannot expect to feel better while holding resentment.
- You can't aspire to improve while holding resentment.
- You can't expect greatness to come from gossiping.
- Give up. You deserve peace, not because they do.
- Freedom is forgiveness. Gossip is enslavement. Slow death is bitterness.
- Take the higher option that focuses on purpose rather than people.

Ultimately, a liberated heart is the loudest triumph, and calmness is the greatest reward.

# 4. The Habit Of Entertaining Toxic People
## *Inviting Chaos Into Your Life*

Pain has an odd kind of generosity; some people continue to give it away, while others keep holding onto it. It always seems courteous, devoted, or "helpful" to entertain poisonous people. In reality, though, it causes crisis, drama, and an ongoing loss of your productivity, peace of mind and sense of purpose. Not only do toxic people cause occasional problems, but they also create a chaotic environment in your life.

You have to be brutal about one thing if you want to develop, create, and love well: who you let into your inner circle.

*"The quality of your life is the quality of your relationships."*
*C. Joy Bell C.*

*"You cannot hang out with negative people and expect to live a positive life."*
*Joel Osteen*

*"Stop letting people who do so little for you control so much of your mind, feelings, and emotions."*
*Unknown*

## The True Meaning of "Toxic":

"Toxic" is more than just a harmful word.

It refers to anything or anyone that slowly inhibits your identity, growth, or happiness.

A poisonous relationship, mindset, or habit is one that: depletes your energy prevents you from moving forward reduces your self-confidence causes tension rather than assistance

Toxicity usually operates in silence. Sometimes it crumbles instead of exploding. One minor adjustment, one disregarded warning sign, one accepted behavior, and all of a sudden your life is full with troubles that you never meant to invite.

## To put it simply:

Anything that causes more harm than good is considered toxic. In reality, you cannot develop in a toxic environment. You need to first identify what is toxic and then have the will to get rid of, replace, or overcome it if you want to grow, rise, and realize your full potential.

"Toxic" is a pattern rather than a clinical diagnosis. A harmful individual regularly: invalidates how you feel (minimizes, dismisses pain). depletes your energy (drama, neediness, and persistent negativity). manipulates or controls (blame-shifting, guilt-tripping). disregards boundaries (invades privacy, arrives late, and breaches promises).

Toxicity thrives on chaos by inciting conflict, stirring up trouble, and avoiding accountability. Not everyone who hurts you is toxic. People make mistakes. Toxicity is an ongoing pattern and habit that, if disregarded, can be dangerous.

**Why do people always Invite Them In:**

It's easy to believe that "saving" or "sticking by" individuals makes us good. However, we constantly retain toxic individuals around for the following reasons:

1. Fear of being alone or of conflict. We would prefer to put up with unpleasant company than an awkward conversation or a dull evening.

2. History and duty: Long-standing connections or family ties make it more difficult to stop a relationship, even when it is clear that it is unhealthy.

3. Neglect and hope: We reminisce about the happy times and persuade ourselves that change is on the way.

4. seeking approval: Drama attracts attention, which is why some people want it, and we encourage it by reacting and acceptance.

Admitting any of these causes is not embarrassing, but when they develop into a habit, they become risky.

**The Price of Toxic Hosting:**

In addition to making you unhappy, toxic relationships rob you of your future.

Anxiety, low self-esteem and persistent second-guessing are examples of emotional costs.

Physical costs include altered eating habits, stress-related health problems, and poor sleep.

Relational costs include damaged friendships, reduced family ties, and a decline in trust.

Time lost, creative blockages, and unfulfilled objectives are examples of productivity costs.

Spiritual costs include despair, a lack of faith in people, and the draining of energy.

You don't realize the harm until the floor gives way, thus entertaining toxic people is similar to inviting termites into your home.

**When "Helping" Turns Into Harm:**

Supporting someone is not the same as contributing to their chaos. It is not necessary to be a doormat to be caring. You are no longer assisting; rather, you are complicit if your support consistently permits harmful decisions (addictive behavior, abuse, manipulation).

Does my engagement improve them, or does it increase their reliance on drama? This is the question of true help. If the latter, taking a step back might be the healthiest option.

## How to Put an End to Entertaining Toxic People (Doable Steps):

1.  Examine your circle. List the ten persons you spend the most time with. Note whether you feel energized, neutral, exhausted, or anxious after making contact with each. The medicine in this checklist is completely truthful.

2.  Describe what is not negotiable. Determine what you will not put up with: persistent lying, rudeness, deceit, or violence. Action is made simple by transparency.

3.  Establish and uphold clear boundaries. "I can't participate in conversations where you insult people," you might say. Then, if the behavior persists, leave. Boundaries are declarations of self-respect, not threats.

4.  When things become tough, use scripts.

    ***"I don't accept being spoken to that way, even though I care about you."***

    ***"I'm not available for drama at this time."***

    ***"I'm deciding to take a back seat until things improve."***

5.  Don't destroy your character; instead, restrict access. Cutting someone out does not imply that you want them to suffer. It indicates that you won't let their drama become the norm for you. Reduce time first, and if nothing changes, proceed to deeper isolation.

6. Use constructive habits in place of interaction. Take a stroll, write for fifteen minutes, call a friend who is in good health, or work intently for thirty minutes if you want to respond to an angry message.

7. Keep social media safe. Restrict, mute, or unfollow accounts that cause you anxiety. A modern practice that safeguards your mental space is digital detox.

**Specific Situations: Workplace & Family Toxicity:**

Family: Loyalty to your family is noble, but it shouldn't come at the price of your spirit. Establish limits gradually at first; if they are consistently disregarded, set emotional or physical boundaries. It is possible to love at a distance. Living a safe life is self-serving.

Workplace: When superiors or coworkers are toxic, record their actions, refrain from gossiping, report them to HR, or devise a plan for leaving. Moving professionally toward a better atmosphere can sometimes be the best plan of action.

**The Inner Work: Why Boundaries Don't Work (And How to Make Them Work):**

Boundaries break down when we:

1. Lack belief (we don't think we deserve better).

2. Desire acceptance (we are more afraid of rejection than we are of growth).

3. Repeat past behaviors because, despite the pain, we find safety in the familiar.

4. Strengthen self-worth rituals, such as daily affirmations, short-term victories (completing a task), tiny gestures of self-care, and reminding yourself that you are not accountable for the brokenness of others.

**When It's Time to Cut the Connection:**

Safety is the measure at times. Cutting ties is required if the relationship involves abuse, addiction that puts you in danger, persistent deception, or persistent betrayal despite efforts to reform. Cutting off is courage, not cruelty. You are picking life over disaster.

**How to build a healthy circle:**

- Make an effort :

    Invite those that enrich your life with zest, insight, and warmth.

- Promote reciprocity :

    In a healthy relationship, both parties give and receive.

- Put money into sustaining groups:

    Classes, church small groups, book clubs, and creative groups all bring together people with similar interests.

- Set an example of the behavior you want:

Be the kind of friend you wish to have: trustworthy, reliable, supportive.

- Coping with regret and Isolation Following the Cut :

  Feeling guilty or lonely after getting rid of toxic people is common. The cost of freedom is in discomfort. Remember this:

Responsibility is not the same as guilt. While responsibility is an action you take when something is genuinely your fault, guilt can be an echo of your concerns.

Peace endures; loneliness is brief. Make the most of your time by engaging in meaningful activities and forming new connections.

**Daily Habits to Prevent Conflict :**

**Boundary check in the morning**

Remind yourself of your limitations first thing in the morning.

**Check at the end of the day:**

Take note of the interactions that made you feel better vs those that made you feel worse. Make the necessary adjustments.

**Stoplight for views:**

Red means to leave. Yellow indicates a defined limit. Green means "engage." Before each interaction, use it.

**Reminder cleanup every week:**

Examine your list of relationships and make any necessary changes.

**Closing the Benefit of Cleaner Air:**

Removing toxic people out of your life is a process of purification rather than punishment. Imagine being able to breathe better air after years of smoking. You will develop more quickly, have better sleep, think more clearly, and love more freely. The only resources you cannot reclaim are your time, focus, and emotional energy. Consider them precious.

It is not withdrawal to leave a chaotic situation. It is deciding to live up to a higher level. It's deciding to stop becoming the starting point for other people's drama.

Decide who you will no longer entertain today. Determine who should be seated at your table. Make the decision that your life is too valuable to be noisy.

Put money into developing groups: Classes, church small groups, book clubs, and mastermind groups all bring together like-minded individuals.

Set an example of the behavior you want. Be the kind of friend you wish to have: trustworthy, reliable, supportive, and on time.

# 5. The Habit Of Impulsive Spending

## *When Your Wallet Has No Brakes*

*"Do not save what is left after spending, but spend what is left after saving."*

### *Warren Buffett*

Although many people view money as a source of stress and temptation, it is also a source of power. One of the most obvious yet harmful behaviors that keeps people in a financial crisis is impulsive spending. It starts small, a cappuccino here, a fancy device there until all of a sudden your wallet and bank account feels like it has no brakes.

Emotional triggers, such as the urge to impress, the need to avoid stress, or the promise of instant gratification, are often the source of impulse purchases. The harsh reality is that every dollar you spend aimlessly is a support for someone else's dream rather than your own.

**The Economic Impact of Impulsive Purchases:**

1. leaving you unprepared for crises and depleting your funds.

2. causes regret and guilt, which always results in further bad choices.

3. prevents you from accumulating wealth and keeps you reliant on the cycle of earning and spending.

4. makes you a passive observer of life, living paycheck to paycheck rather than achieving financial freedom.

What's the worst? Hardly does impulsive spending lead to long-term happiness. It provides short-term pleasure rather than long-term fulfillment.

**Think about it:**

Analyze this:

- Why did I purchase this? Was it emotional or necessary?
- Do I spend money to genuinely meet my needs or to impress others?
- If I saved this money instead, how would my life be different?
- Does this purchase help me get out of debt or keep me in debt?

The first step to regaining your financial control is to honestly respond to these.

**How to Develop Financial Self-Control:**

**1. First, emergency savings:**

Make a safety net, no matter how little. $500–$1000 helps avoid impulsive borrowing and cover unforeseen costs. Savings should be viewed as an unavoidable expense. Before making any further purchases, pay it.

## 2. A Strategic Budget :

Keep tabs on your earnings and spending. Understand just where your money is going. Set aside money for investments, needs, and wants. Allow for minor joys, but refrain from guilt-driven purchases.

## 3. Make Future Investments:

Over time, every dollar invested compounds. Big rewards come from small and regular investments. Invest in stocks, mutual funds, or retirement accounts to make money work for you rather than wasting it on pointless items.

## 4. Avoid Spending to Make an Impression:

The trap is social pressure. Purchasing items to flaunt to those who are not fortunate themselves can quickly lead to financial distress.

Simple daily activities can change your financial situation: Instead of dining out, pack a lunch. Wait a full day before purchasing to reduce impulsive purchases.

## 5. Little effort, big gains :

Simple daily activities can change your financial situation: Instead of dining out, pack a lunch. Wait a full day before purchasing to reduce impulsive purchases. Save money automatically; just set it and forget about it.

*"Do not go where the path may lead, go instead where there is no path and leave a trail."*
**Ralph Waldo Emerson**

Being financially independent is a decision. Whether you choose to invest, save, or spend prudently, every choice you make today is a step closer to becoming independent. Over time, every little action adds up. Your little effort today will pay off significantly later.

**Picture a life in which**:

You don't worry about unforeseen expenses.

Rather than attempting to impress outsiders, you invest in your dreams.

You feel in charge of both your life and your finances. This is the kind of life that financial discipline produces. It is deliberate rather than instant.

**Avoiding Impulsive Purchases :**

Make a list of what you need vs what you want. Purchase only items that support your financial objectives.

1. Delay Gratification: Hold off on making a purchase. Don't buy if the desire goes away.

2. Limit Access: Cut back on online shopping apps, unsubscribe from advertisements, and unfollow businesses.

3. Reward Yourself Sensibly: Reward yourself with modest, well-thought-out gifts rather than careless spending.

4. Educate Yourself: Being financially literate allows you to take control of your finances rather than let them control you.

**Final thoughts:**

*"Wealth consists not in having great possessions, but in having few wants."*

*Epictetus*

Gaining your freedom, calm, and power is more important than simply saving money when you break the habit of impulsive buying. You are teaching your body, mind, and soul that you are in charge every time you choose discipline over want.

Financial freedom is determined by how purposefully you invest and spend your money, not by how much you earn. Start small, maintain consistency, and see how little efforts can lead to significant improvements in your life.

**The lesson:**

Your wallet has brakes. You can decide whether or not to use them. Increase your wealth, safeguard your peace of mind, and create a life that fulfills you rather than fulfills the passing desires of the present.

# As I Wrap Up This Book

Dear friends,

I want you to inhale deeply and consider all that these pages have shown you as we wrap up this narrative in print. This book has taught you something many people don't discover until it's too late: poisonous habits destroy lives, not just days.

We started by revealing the quiet saboteurs of the mind:

- Negative self-talk that makes you shrink...
- Delaying your dreams due to procrastination
- The comfort trap of inactivity destroys your drive.
- These damaging habits go unnoticed.
- They slowly erode your possibilities until you look back and realize you lost years to habits you never addressed.

Next, we addressed the lifestyle and health killers: sedentary behavior, sleep deprivation, long-term stress, substance misuse, neglecting mental health, screen time, and unhealthy food habits.

These behaviors deplete your energy, impair your mental capacity, accelerate your body's aging, and reduce your life expectancy.

The relationship and life drainers that we found were: disrespect, entitlement, deception, infidelity, gossip, anger, entertaining toxic individuals, and reckless spending.

These behaviors ruin trust, poison love, and block your potential to achieve stability.

However, we also need to be aware of the following silent bad habits:

- The drive to chase attention and approval
- Seeking approval all the time destroys your identity:
- Attempting to impress individuals who don't care about you makes you lose yourself.

Be who you are. Remain true to who you are. You don't require approval from everyone.

*The sexual indiscipline habit*

- Your body shouldn't be accessible to everyone.
- Destinies have been ruined by fleeting pleasure and comfort.
- Your future is safeguarded by discipline. Self-control is the first step toward stability.

*The tendency to commit crimes and take short cuts*

- Avoid committing the crime if you don't want to do your sentence.
- The quick life is devoid of progress.
- Shortcuts destroy futures.

Real riches are the result of perseverance, effort, and dedication; quick money vanishes like smoke.

*The addiction to gambling, clubbing, and masturbation*

- Addictions silently kill growth.
- They deplete your vitality, self-control, concentration, and future.
- The basic truth is that what you starve dies, what you feed thrives.
- Give up your addictions. Feed your mission.
- Addictions are like chains.

Additionally, chains are used for slaves. However, dear friends, you are not a slave.

# The Basic Message Of This Book

Toxic habits create toxic lives, as this book has openly and clearly demonstrated. They damage your future, steal your energy, cloud your wisdom, and hinder your progress.

However, this is the most important fact:

- You can escape.
- Rebuilding is possible.
- You have control over toxic habits.

Swap damaging behaviors for uplifting ones:

- Read intellectually uplifting books.
- Make connections with those who motivate and push you.
- Invest in your long-term goals.
- Develop self-control
- Be patient.
- Gain emotional stability

These are the behaviors that promote advancement, stability, and peace.

# The Call To Action

*Be disciplined to protect your future.*

*Use self-control to safeguard your fate.*

*Reject poisonous behaviors to keep your peace.*

*Even if someone else succeeds before you, it does not imply that you are failing.*

*Everybody has their own schedule.*

*Continue to push. It's almost payday.*

*One life is all you got :*

*Don't waste another year making the same horrible errors in bad habits.*

*Give up the behaviors that are keeping you hostage.*

*Your mission, your aspirations, and your family all depend on you being strong.*

*Don't allow destructive behaviors to rob you of your abilities.*

*This is your time.*

*This is your opportunity.*

*This is a fresh start for you.*

*avoid shortcuts :*

*Build your future responsibly and slowly.*

*Put logic ahead of desire.*

*Pick order over disorder.*

*Prioritize stability over brief enjoyment.*

*You will not only succeed but also rule your life if you break free from your destructive habits.*

*Today is the beginning of your new life.*

*Enter it.*

*And now, at last :*

*Here is my roadmap, which I present to you in good faith, and I sincerely hope it will help you overcome and become unstoppable.*

*A road map for overcoming toxic habits and becoming your true self.*

# Resources For Further Reading

*"Every small choice is a vote for the person you are becoming."*
***Atomic Habits — James Clear***

*"When you understand your habit loop, you gain the power to rewrite your behavior."*

***The Power of Habit — Charles Duhigg***

*"Make it tiny so your mind cannot resist it."*

***Tiny Habits — BJ Fogg***

*"What you repeat in private becomes your result in public."*

***The Slight Edge — Jeff Olson***

*"The mountain you fight is often the past you refuse to release."*

***The Mountain Is You — Brianna Wiest***

*"Healing begins the moment you choose responsibility over excuses."*

***The Road Less Traveled — M. Scott Peck***

*"Pain stored in the body can shape habits you don't even realize you have."*

***The Body Keeps the Score — Bessel van der Kolk***

*"Recovery begins when you stop negotiating with your excuses."*
***Quit Like a Woman — Holly Whitaker***

*"Your life becomes lighter every time you let go of what doesn't matter."*

### Essentialism — Greg McKeown

*"Own your morning, and you reclaim your life."*

### The 5 AM Club — Robin Sharma

### Resources for your personal growth :

www.unlimitedtofail.com

www.**tinybuddha.com**

**www.**mindbodygreen.com

www.www.psychologytoday.com/us

www.tonyogbemure

# About The Author

Tony Ogbemure is a motivational speaker, coach, blogger, freelance writer, and author passionate about helping people overcome limiting habits and achieve personal growth. His books, Beyond Limits and the recently published Toxic Habits: Roadmap to rise above, Break Free, Become Unstoppable, encourage readers to face harmful habits, accept responsibility, and reach their full potential.

There are several ways to get in touch with Tony Ogbemure and keep up with his work:

Telephone: (618) 381-1505

Email: info@unlimitedtofail.com | dominionionreign094@gmail.com

tonyttm094@gmail.com

Blog: unlimitedtofail.com

www.tonyogbemure.com is the author's website.

www.ingramcontent.com/pod-product-compliance
Lightning Source LLC
Chambersburg PA
CBHW061649120626
46550CB00003B/878